PENGUIN BOOKS

THE BLOODSTAINED THRONE

BABURAM ACHARYA, the first and only historian laureate of Nepal, was a scholar and researcher who pioneered the writing of Nepalese history based on indigenous resources. He is credited with coining the Nepali name 'Sagarmatha' for Mt Everest, the world's tallest mountain. An honorary member of the Royal Nepal Academy, he was awarded the Tribhuvan Award in 1963.

He wrote fourteen books (seven published posthumously) and over one hundred research-based pieces and articles on subjects ranging from Nepalese history to Nepal–China relations. He is best known for his four-volume biography of King Prithvinarayan Shah, the founder of modern Nepal, and *Aba Yasto Kahilyai Nahos*, a collection of his essays.

SHREEKRISHNA ACHARYA, seventy-five, holds two master's degrees. He taught astronomy and Nepali literature at the Balmiki Vidyapeeth of Tribhuvan University, Kathmandu. Writer and editor of books, he also served as the vice chancellor of Nepal's Mahendra Sanskrit University. He is the son of Nepalese historian Baburam Acharya.

MADHAV ACHARYA, the grandson of Baburam Acharya, served as the Kathmandu-based correspondent of Kyodo News of Japan for over three decades. He also worked with the state-run Radio Nepal as a broadcaster, and with RSS, Nepal's national news network, as an executive editor. Besides, he edited the now-defunct English-language newspaper *The Motherland*.

THE
BLOODSTAINED THRONE
STRUGGLES FOR POWER IN NEPAL
(1775–1914)

BABURAM ACHARYA

EDITED BY
SHREEKRISHNA ACHARYA

TRANSLATED BY
MADHAV ACHARYA

PENGUIN BOOKS
An imprint of Penguin Random House

PENGUIN BOOKS

USA | Canada | UK | Ireland | Australia
New Zealand | India | South Africa | China | Singapore

Penguin Books is part of the Penguin Random House group of companies
whose addresses can be found at global.penguinrandomhouse.com

Published by Penguin Random House India Pvt. Ltd
4th Floor, Capital Tower 1, MG Road,
Gurugram 122 002, Haryana, India

Penguin
Random House
India

First published by Penguin Books India 2013

ISBN 9780143416371

Typeset in Garamond by R. Ajith Kumar, New Delhi
Printed at Repro India Limited

www.penguin.co.in

MIX
Paper from
responsible sources
FSC® C047271

Contents

Contents

Editor's Note

My father, *Itihas Shiromani* (Historian Laureate) Baburam Acharya, wrote several essays and articles on manifold aspects of Nepal and walks of Nepalese life, published in scattered forms during his lifetime. A few of his writings remained unpublished. Attempts are being made to bring out in book form, and on genre-basis, some of his published and unpublished works. This volume marks the beginning of such an endeavour.

The late Baburam Acharya had conducted in-depth research, studies and analysis in various fields and areas of Nepal and the Nepalese, including the country's history, geography, archaeology, culture, language, literature, and other arts. These works step beyond the realm of the ordinary also because they had been carried out during the intolerant Rana regime, when any interest shown in acquiring knowledge about the nation's history could be construed as a punishable act of prying into politics. Baburam's research and studies had unveiled facts and truths that are of great significance even today. It is hoped that these works help to enlighten the readers about the past of Nepal and her people.

His life of want and poverty did not dissuade the eminent historian from his research and investigative studies, nor did it deter him from fulfilling what can best be described as his heightened sense of responsibility to the nation. All the writings of this collection were produced after Baburam lost his eyesight.

This volume has ten historical pieces, all written for broadcast over Radio Nepal on request from the then officials of the country's only broadcasting institution, which has meant that, occasionally, they tend to read like narratives tailored for broadcasting. At times, they also smack of repetition, but that is because we have pieced together essays and articles produced at different periods of time. Only a few of these have been published. Whether or not a particular piece had been previously published is indicated at the end of each chapter.

King Prithvinarayan Shah had successfully driven the aggressive and irreverent British out of Nepal. But after his rule and that of his able son Prince Bahadur Shah, the Nepalese seemed to have lost the capacity and courage to face events and situations squarely. They also seem to have lost their pride in patriotism and in the Nepalese character of fearlessness. All the Nepalese *bhardar*s (courtiers or members of the Council of Nobility) seemed to be indulgent and interested only in accumulating wealth, wallowing in debauchery and enjoying the pleasures of life. While machinations, murders and massacre became the order of the day in Nepal, the whole of Europe saw the dawn of the Industrial Revolution, bolstered by which the Europeans went about colonizing various parts of the world. Conscious citizens of colonized Asia and Africa had begun to come out openly in strong revolts against colonialism. But in Nepal the people were forced to endure hardships and exploitation at the hands of home-grown autocrats. Though an uneasy calm prevailed in the country, illiteracy and poverty were widespread; starvation, too, was a reality. And none from the ruling clique showed any concern, let alone made any attempt to mitigate the suffering of the people. The autocrats had not cared to conceive of any plan for the growth and progress of the country, or for the comfort and happiness of the people. Comfort and amenities of life remained mostly confined to the privileged high-class families. Nepal's general condition during that period may well account for her present-day maladies, including her grinding poverty and backwardness.

The articles of this collection seek to convey the message that Nepal should no longer be the playground of disdainful murders and conspiracies, and her people no longer—and never again—should be subjected to the tyranny of autocracy.

This work seeks to unveil the actual facts and happenings in Nepal's history. It does not aim to criticize or level charges, nor is there an attempt to sow hatred or malice against anyone; indeed, for that matter, this work is also not directed towards any undeserved eulogy or encomium. The publication of this collection would become meaningful if it helped to instil a sense of nationalism among the proud and patriotic Nepalese people, besides sharing with curious and intelligent readers a few insights into the nation's past.

Shreekrishna Acharya
Editor/Publisher

17 November 1998

Translator's Note

In undertaking this translation, my only objective was to take my grandfather's works to the English-reading public. I have tried, as far as I could, to convey the essential meaning of his words and expressions in simple English. In rendering this work, which is far removed from us both in time and space, there were times when I was tempted to paraphrase, for lack of clarity; but I think I did resist. Yet, faults have crept in, and those I must accept as mine.

Rendering names, titles and historical terms was difficult. The traditional method of referring names by surname in the second or third reference was inapplicable, as it would only lead to confusion. For example, Jungbahadur Rana could not be referred to by his family name in the second or third references because other characters too happen to bear Rana as their surname, and are frequently mentioned on the same page, if not in the same paragraph. Ditto with the surname Shah. At the same time, giving the name in full in all references would have been redundant. So, for clarity's sake and to make it more intelligible, I have used the first name, not surname, starting with the second reference. As for the titles, these are essentially Nepalese titles having no English equivalents. So I have tried to go for the nearest equivalents. Regarding the historical terms, I have tried to set down what is the most likely meaning.

Bikash Sangraula helped a great deal by reviewing the text of the translation and taking the work to the esteemed publishing house.

Madhav Acharya
Kathmandu, Nepal

One

The Tragic End of Prince Bahadur Shah

When King Prithvinarayan Shah named his newborn prince Pratapsingh Shah, he harboured the hope that his eldest son would be like the famous Mewad king Rana Pratapsingh Shah, who was known for his bravery and skills in warfare. But, as time rolled by, this hope was belied. Prithvi's younger son Bahadur Shah, however, lived up to his expectations. Bahadur Shah was a seventeen-year-old bachelor at the time of Prithvinarayan's death. Since childhood the prince had always been alongside his father; he was well versed in the nitty-gritty of politics and had also acquired battlefield skills and experience. He had stayed away from debauchery and indulgence, showing signs of industriousness, bravery and courage right at an early stage of his life.

With conquests in the east almost fully achieved, Prithvinarayan had set his eyes on similar success in his campaign in the west and had, in the process, camped at Nuwakot. However, at this point of time, he suddenly fell ill. Earlier, his younger brother Soorpratap Shah had deserted him, disappearing in Kaski, leaving the Gorkha province. Another brother, Mahoddamkirti Shah, had also developed differences with Prithvi, which led him to flee and take shelter with the King of Kaski, who was known for his antagonism towards the Gorkhalis. These developments had given everyone the jitters, from Prithvi himself to Pratapsingh (who was staying in Kathmandu) and Bahadur Shah, as well as other nobles and courtiers. King Prithvi succumbed to his illness in Nuwakot on 10 January 1775, paving the way for Pratapsingh to wear the royal crown in Kathmandu.

The escape of Mahoddamkirti sowed seeds of unease in the mind of the new king. He feared that his younger brother Bahadur Shah, aided and abetted by his uncles, would rise in revolt against him in the Choubise states (collective name given to twenty-four tiny states, also known as principalities, of the time in Nepal). The suspicion may have been uncalled for; yet, in consultation with his principal adviser Brajanath Pandit and the likes of Swaroopsingh Karki, Pratapsingh went on to put his uncle Daljit Shah and brother Bahadur Shah in confinement; this was done while the latter was still mourning his father's death in Nuwakot. Daljit fled later, which resulted in the confiscation of his property and assets. As for Bahadur Shah, he performed the post-death rites of his father while still in detention.

The late Prithvi had posted Pandit Gajaraj Mishra in Benaras as a permanent Nepalese agent, in order to keep himself abreast of the political developments taking place in neighbouring India. Both of Prithvi's sons, the new King Pratapsingh and his brother Bahadur Shah, were among Gajaraj's beloved and devoted disciples. When he visited Nepal to offer blessings to the new king, he found to his utter dismay and sadness that his other beloved disciple, the king's brother, had been placed under house arrest. Gajaraj proceeded to plead on behalf of Bahadur Shah, saying that the imprisoned prince was entitled to a life of freedom even if it was to be somewhere in exile. Unable to ignore his guru's forceful plea, Pratapsingh lifted the orders of house arrest on Bahadur Shah who quickly moved over to Bettiya, India, to start living in exile.

But life as an exile in no way diminished Bahadur Shah's sense of loyalty and dutifulness towards his country. Patriotism was in his blood. He kept his mind constantly occupied with the need for the further advancement of the unification campaign initiated by his illustrious father. Based on the information he had received in exile, Bahadur Shah wrote a letter to Pratapsingh, saying: 'The firangis are about to launch an attack on Chitwan; hence a pre-emptive attack may well be in order.' The letter prompted a timely intervention by Nepal, which was able to take control of Chitwan rather easily. However, barely three months after celebrating the Chitwan victory, Pratapsingh, only twenty-six, suddenly died an untimely death, leaving behind his only son, Ranabahadur Shah, a two-year-old at the time. Thus, the infant prince ascended the Nepalese throne on 16 December 1777.

It was Ranabahadur's mother, Queen Rajendralaxmi, who was affected the most by the unexpected demise of her husband. Pratapsingh's other wife Maijumaharani was expecting at this time, so she could not be asked to perform Sati. Brajanath Pandit was already hatching a plot wherein

Rajendralaxmi would burn herself at Pratapsingh's pyre. Brajanath knew that if that were to happen, he could realize his dream of becoming the ruler of Nepal, albeit in a de facto capacity, as the king was only an infant. [It is not clear in the article, but one surmises that Brajanath was outwitted by the widowed queen, who managed to avoid having to commit Sati.]

All the responsibilities of running the affairs of the recently unified kingdom now fell on the queen's shoulders. While the task of unification itself was yet to be completed, there was much more to be done in terms of administrative reforms in those provinces which had already been won over. The queen found herself in a situation where she had nobody close to trust or in whom she could confide. So, she had no option but to recall her brother-in-law, Bahadur Shah, from exile. Actually, she couldn't have found a closer kin and a heartier well-wisher of both herself and her son Ranabahadur than Bahadur Shah. The queen sent out a letter recalling Bahadur Shah from exile. Upon receiving the letter, the prince promptly departed for Kathmandu. But, for an unexplained reason, he was held up in the Terai until the purification rites (the post-death mourning rites of Pratapsingh Shah) were completed in Kathmandu where his uncle Daljit Shah performed all the rituals, including that of feeding rice to the dead. A few days later, Bahadur Shah returned to Kathmandu after affixing his signature on a *dharmapatra* (a bond of pledge and commitment); then, with the consent of his sister-in-law Rajendralaxmi, he assumed the title of 'chautara' (a title bestowed on a royal relative authorizing him with the power to take decisions on behalf of the state). Thereby, Bahadur Shah found himself firmly in charge of the kingdom.

Then, first of all, the brother-in-law and sister-in-law, working in tandem, decided to suppress the non-Gorkhalis who had effectively taken control of the durbar. Brajanath Pandit was arrested on the charge of being involved in the 'evil act of bringing physical harm to the king'; he was subsequently deported from the country, his head tonsured, and caste downgraded. Sirdar Parasuram Thapa was thrown into prison, while Swaroopsingh Karki, a minister, escaped retribution, having already fled the country. Later, Bahadur Shah and his sister-in-law formed the new Courtiers' Council through mutual consultations.

For the next five months, close and amicable relations prevailed between the two. Bahadur Shah desperately wanted to invade the state of Tanahun as soon as possible—this was in line with his illustrious father's plan. Rajendralaxmi, however, baulked at the idea. At this point of time, she seems to have harboured the notion that once her son came of age, it would be he who would advance the cause of the unification campaign. Bahadur Shah, however, was averse to the idea of letting time slip by unnecessarily. He was also seething with the desire to 'outstrip the power of the British'. Over this a dispute arose between him and Rajendralaxmi; then the latter, aided by Sarbajit Rana, interned Bahadur Shah at the royal palace. Once again, Gajaraj Mishra returned from Benaras and in a bid to mend fences, secured the release of Bahadur Shah. But this time the queen kept to herself the reins of control of the administration, and Bahadur Shah was left virtually powerless.

Meanwhile, Rajendralaxmi was seen moving about freely in public places though the mourning period for her dead husband was not yet over. Senior and influential palace nobles and courtiers viewed with disdain the queen's horse-riding trips out of the royal palace, accompanied by women attendants who were also on horseback. Rumours that she was involved in an illicit relationship with Minister Sarbajit Rana began making the rounds in the palace circles. For his part, Bahadur Shah made good use of the situation to re-establish his authority. Winning over a palace official, Shriharsha Pant, at the initiative of his uncle Daljit, and with the aid of a few male servants at the palace, Sarbajit was slain in one of the palace basements. The queen mother was placed under 'respectful' house arrest, and the younger son of Prithvinarayan Shah once again successfully assumed control of the administration, on 2 September 1778.

At this time, Bahadur Shah had committed an unpardonable blunder. He could be forgiven for holding Rajendralaxmi under house arrest over differences on plans and principles, but the brutal beheading of senior courtier Sarbajit went against the very grain of his father's dictum that 'one's own brothers and courtiers should never ever be killed'. So, the slaying of Sarbajit was an act that could not be pardoned. Moreover, Sarbajit's murder marked the beginning of the despicable practice of assassination and massacre of nobles and courtiers at the Nepalese durbar, setting in motion a sequence of vicious events like the infamous Kot Massacre, which is believed to have pushed the kingdom towards a century-long era of darkness.

Soon after taking control of the administration, Bahadur Shah began preparations to conquer the province of Tanahun; a few months later, he emerged victorious. In the meantime, Rajendralaxmi was also not sitting idle; she was no less audacious, and certainly not a gutless, innocent woman. While Bahadur Shah was in Gorkha to consolidate the conquest of Tanahun, she secured assistance from a prominent palace courtier Balabhadra Shah to quickly send out people to call back the senior chautara and Prince Mahoddamkirti Shah and Brajanath Pandit. Brajanath fought shy of a prompt return, but Mahoddamkirti wasted no time in reporting himself back to the palace. Daljit, Prithvi's younger brother, and Balabhadra Shah, who had been asked to keep watch on the activities of the queen, failed to check Mahoddamkirti's advancement in the corridors of power—he went on to take effective control of even the Courtiers' Council. A drama was enacted to render justice to the queen and to prove her innocence of any wrongdoing. Thus, courtesy Mahoddamkirti, not only was Rajendralaxmi released from house arrest, but the control of the administration was also wrested for her from the hands of Bahadur Shah, on 20 June 1779.

Following this unexpected turn of events, Daljit fled Kathmandu; he also masterminded the escape of Bahadur Shah, who was then in Gorkha. Meanwhile, at the Kathmandu durbar, Shriharsha Pant was accused of framing false charges against the queen; his lips were burnt and he was subsequently deported. Moreover, two courtiers were put to death, trampled by elephants, while two others bled to their death after being impaled by sharp iron stakes. Thereafter, the queen appointed

Bandhu Rana, a brother of Sarbajit's, and Devdutt Thapa as ministers.

The family feud at the durbar in Kathmandu led to a shortfall in Nepalese soldiers stationed in the hilly parts of the Tanahun province, thus enabling the king there to regain control of his lost state rather easily. Not long after, Mahoddamkirti was charged with slaughtering a Brahmin, and was deported. Gajaraj Mishra, based in Benaras, who often took Bahadur Shah's side, was fired from his post, and replaced by Brajanath on the orders of the queen.

With all the hurdles out of her way, Rajendralaxmi began living a life of pleasure and debauchery. Meanwhile, as Bahadur Shah had been pushed out of the country and as an indulgent queen was running the affairs of the state, Bamsaraj Pande of Gorkha and Shivanarayan Khatri of Maajh-Kirat arrived at the conclusion that the onerous task of expanding the kingdom could no longer be carried out and so they fled Nepal. While Rajendralaxmi shed no tears at their escape, the kings of the other provinces who were opposed to the Nepalese kingdom started plotting against Nepal. In their eyes, a hapless woman had again taken control of the state administration, thereby rendering it weak and inefficient. In the east, the widow of King Karna Sen of Kirat Pradesh was devising a plan to regain her lost state. The fugitive Swaroopsingh Karki, who had fled Nepal, was helping her in this objective. In the west, the Choubise kings were already making preparations to invade the Nepalese kingdom.

Nepal faced the crucial question of how to defend itself when the Choubise states moved in a planned and coordinated manner. All the Nepalese nobles and courtiers as well as the military assembled in Kathmandu and later departed for Gorkha with the intent of defending the province. A fierce battle took place between the soldiers of the Choubise states and the Nepalese troops at Siranchowk-Gadhi. Around 200 soldiers of the Choubise states were wiped out, while the Nepalese side lost only fifteen lives. In the end, the army of the Choubise states was forced to back out. In the aftermath of the battle, with their strength considerably dwindled, the Choubise states started feuding among themselves. The battle took place on 4 February 1782.

At this time, King Siddhinarayan Shah of Kaski, one of the Choubise states, went on to take the side of the Nepalese kingdom. This angered King Birmardan Shah of Lamjung, who, assembling the defeated Choubise soldiers, mounted an unexpected invasion on Kaski and conquered it. The Nepalese courtiers were then compelled to plot an attack on Lamjung in order to win back the state for the Kaski king who had stood by the Nepalese side. Rajendralaxmi gave her consent to the invasion and, towards this end, recalled Bamsaraj from exile to take part in the campaign. She also appointed Damodar Pande, a brother of Bamsaraj's, as minister. Under the leadership of Bamsaraj, the Nepalese Army conquered Lamjung rather easily—the state merged into the Nepalese kingdom on 29 October 1782. Later, the Kaski state voluntarily accepted the suzerainty of the Kingdom of Nepal after entering into a treaty with it.

At this time, the Sen King of Palpa, too, had become an opponent of the Nepalese kingdom; so Rajendralaxmi gave her consent to subdue this state too. Swaroopsingh Karki, after fleeing Nepal, had first taken shelter in Palpa; then he had moved eastward to join the widow of Karna Sen in her plot against Nepal. Rajendralaxmi, following the advice of her close courtiers, decided to entrust Swaroopsingh with the campaign on Palpa, and called him back to Kathmandu.

Bhim Khawas had been involved as a mere soldier when Nepal fought the Choubise kings in the battle of Siranchowk. With the war over, he made it to the position of one of the close attendants of Rajendralaxmi; later, rather unexpectedly, he even became a minister. This irked Bamsaraj Pande who had eyed this ministerial position—he believed he was the rightful claimant on account of being a scion of an illustrious family of Gorkha, and the son of Kalu Pande, an ex-minister. He was also irked by the queen's reinstatement of Swaroopsingh Karki, a man once known for his anti-Gorkhali posture. When the queen heard about Bamsaraj's resentment, she had him deported from the country. This was on 27 December 1783.

With the return of Swaroopsingh, a plan was afoot to establish authority over the states of Palpa and Parbat, and also to invade other Choubise states, one by one. The Nepalese Army fully involved itself in what was then called the Victory Campaign. Unfortunately, however, at this very point of time, symptoms that the queen had fallen victim to tuberculosis began to surface. In exasperation, she now began to concentrate more on ensuring a secure future for her infant son than on the campaign. To this end, Daljit Shah was called back to Kathmandu and reinstated as a minister.

At this point of time, Prince Ranabahadur was one year

short of the right age for *bratabandha* (sacred-thread-wearing ceremony). But a dispirited Rajendralaxmi decided to perform the auspicious ritual ahead of time and, with that intent, visited Gorkha, accompanied by all the nobles and courtiers. Bahadur Shah, living in exile, was also invited to attend the ceremony. He accepted the invitation thinking that the queen had changed her mind about him. Also called back from exile was Bamsaraj, but for him to go to Gorkha directly would be out of the question as Swaroopsingh, one of his adversaries, continued to hold sway in the Gorkha durbar. Most hesitantly, he returned to Kathmandu on 9 March 1785. But less than a month and a half later, he faced a horrendous charge and was beheaded at the Bhandarkhaal Garden of the royal palace, on the night of 21 April 1785. Bahadur Shah, who returned to Kathmandu from Gorkha along with Rajendralaxmi on completion of the coming-of-age ceremony, was deeply anguished and disturbed by the mysterious murder of Bamsaraj, his principal aide, and a patriot and loyalist to boot. But as he was living under conditions that were akin to a house arrest, Bahadur Shah could not protest—he was forced to stay silent and withdrawn.

Until now, Bahadur Shah had been subjected to considerable torture at the hands of Rajendralaxmi. Consequently, the queen feared and entertained worries that her brother-in-law would act in revenge after her death, deposing her minor son, Ranabahadur Shah. Driven by this thought and with the intent of diminishing Bahadur Shah's powers, she had plotted the murder of Bamsaraj, on the advice of counsellors Bhim Khawas, Garbu Khawas and Swaroopsingh Karki. So, in what could be viewed as phase two of her plan, all of a sudden

Bahadur Shah was arrested, taken to Pharping, about three miles outside the Kathmandu valley, and imprisoned inside a formidable fort. This arrest, his third, took place on 2 July 1786.

Destiny, however, had something different in store for Prithvi's younger son. Just twelve days after this imprisonment, Rajendralaxmi died—on 14 July 1786. This gave rise to a tumultuous time at the royal palace. King Ranabahadur Shah was still a minor, while his uncle Bahadur Shah languished inside a jail in Pharping. Taking advantage of this situation, Bhim Khawas attempted to assume control of the administration, but this was met with stiff resistance from other nobles and courtiers. He had to withdraw and, devoid of any alternative, he collected all his moveable assets and fled the country. Nobody stopped him from leaving.

It is possible that Chautara Balabhadra Shah performed the ten-day death rites of the queen. But since he was only a distant relative, all the priests, nobles and courtiers insisted that the final rites be performed by the closest of kin. So, Bahadur Shah was set free from imprisonment on the tenth day of Rajendralaxmi's death. Accordingly, he performed the eleventh-day rites of *sapindi shraddha* (rice-feeding to the dead) for the queen. Thereafter, with the consent of all the nobles and courtiers, he assumed control of the state administration on 23 July 1786.

Rajendralaxmi was certainly an able administrator. Having stepped into the royal place at a tender age, and with her life mostly spent in the luxuries and pleasures of the Kathmandu durbar, she might not have been very resolute and daring. Yet, during times of crisis, she had shown grit and courage.

That in the course of a power struggle she could outsmart and hold under arrest an ambitious man like Bahadur Shah speaks volumes of her political acumen. But she also showed cowardice—a trait generally attributed to womanhood—by delaying Prithvi's national unification campaign by at least six years. The expansion of the Nepalese kingdom could have been carried out to a great measure had she not been at odds with influential personalities like her brother-in-law Bahadur Shah or if she had accorded priority to the task. Then the credit for unification that Bahadur Shah later came to share would have been hers. Her name would have been written in golden letters in Nepal's history. But suspicion, jealousy and fickleness of mind—again traits generally attributed to womanhood— denied her a cordial relationship with her brother-in-law. The expansion campaign was delayed, leading to a situation wherein Nepal had to incur huge losses. Yet, it was during Rajendralaxmi's rule that the Choubise states towards the west of Gorkha and the east of Kaligandaki were taken within the fold of the Nepalese kingdom. This was no mean achievement. But here it can also be said that the Choubise states were assimilated by default, and not necessarily due to the plans and designs of Rajendralaxmi—the assimilation was achieved because Nepal was compelled to beat back the aggressors.

Swaroopsingh was staying in Kaski when Rajendralaxmi breathed her last. But as soon as Bahadur Shah regained control of the administration, Swaroopsingh was beheaded—on 4 August 1786. The order to put him to death that bore the stamp of the *lalmohar* (the red seal) was purportedly issued by King Ranabahadur. Meanwhile, when the new Courtiers'

Council was formed, there was no place for Balabhadra who had stood by the queen mother all along (he was ousted from the council), while uncle Daljit Shah fled from the kingdom.

Thereafter, as was wont to his nature and attitude, Prince Bahadur Shah began to set his eyes on the Choubise states lying across the Kaligandaki. At this time, almost all the nobles and courtiers were of the view that all the Choubise states across the Kaligandaki should come under Nepal's supremacy with assistance from the Palpa state, which could be procured if Bahadur Shah wedded a princess from there. The prince, however, disagreed. He turned his attention to the Gulmi state, proposing marriage with Vidyalaxmi, a granddaughter of Shiva Shah, the exiled uncle of the King of Gulmi. Arrangements were made for bringing the *dola* (child bride) to Kathmandu and then on to Gorkha, where Bahadur Shah's wedding was solemnized on 20 January 1787.

As planned by Bahadur Shah, one by one all the states across the Kaligandaki—namely, Gulmi, Arghakhanchi, Parbat, Mustang, Musikot, Galkot, Dang, Pyuthan and Jajarkot—came into the fold of the Nepalese kingdom within a few months. After this successful campaign, Kathmandu witnessed a grand victory celebration. Bahadur Shah's popularity grew tremendously.

Spurred by such success, Bahadur Shah embarked on another dangerous game. Alleging that Tibet had stopped trading with Nepal, he launched a sudden attack on Tibet via Kuti and Kerung. The Tibetan Army was no match for the battle-hardened Nepalese Army and it was defeated. Nepal proposed that Tibet 'should either furnish a compensation of ten million rupees or Kuti region should be handed over to Nepal'. The proposal put the Tibetans in a dilemma. Following protracted discussions, an agreement was reached under which Tibet was to give Nepal a tribute of fifty thousand rupees per annum. It was only after this agreement that the Nepalese Army returned home.

As he had already acquired Nepalese citizenship, Shyamarpa Lama, too, had signed the agreement on behalf of Nepal. A Tibetan national, Shyamarpa had earlier fled Tibet after embezzling state funds. His presence to sign the agreement infuriated the Tibetans. Yet, they tolerated it. As pledged by them, the Tibetans paid the tribute of fifty thousand rupees for the first year, but refused to do so for the second year. Instead, they proposed bilateral talks on the matter, and both sides agreed to meet at Kuti Pradesh. But when the Nepalese delegates arrived at the venue they sensed that it was a ruse on the part of the Tibetans to capture and arrest the fugitive Shyamarpa Lama. For his part, Shyamarpa had opted out of the team that went to Kuti Pradesh, perhaps sensing trouble. No sooner had the Nepalese delegates arrived at Kuti than the Tibetans asked why Shyamarpa was missing. Making an issue out of it, they refused to sit down for talks in the absence of the fugitive. By this time, the Nepalese side knew very well what the Tibetans wanted. The Nepalese soldiers accompanying the delegation arrested all the Tibetan delegates, and brought them over to Kathmandu.

By this time, Nepal had extended its territory to the Alaknanda River, taking into its fold Jumla, Dailekh, Dullu, Achham, Bajhang, Doti, Kumaon and Garhwal. In the case of Garhwal, during the Nepalese siege, the ministers of Garhwal, along with their minor king, had taken shelter at a remote fort. For almost a whole year, intermittent fighting ensued between the Nepalese soldiers and the Garhwali forces. Finally, the Nepalese Army was outnumbered and defeated in a small battle at Paniyakhet. As the news of the Nepalese loss spread eastward, the fugitive kings of Kumaon, Doti, Jumla and Achham began to rise against the Nepalese kingdom. The King of Achham promptly returned from exile and brutally killed some two companies of Nepalese soldiers based there. Following the incident, the Nepalese kingdom lost contact with all the states west of Achham, and the Nepalese nobles were left in a quandary.

Prince Bahadur Shah was now facing a grim predicament. While the dispute with Tibet remained unsettled, the kings of the west, who had once been vanquished, were now rising in revolt. And towards the west, only a military campaign had been conducted—the task of administrative reforms was yet to be fulfilled. As the Tibetans continued to remain stubborn, the Nepalese Army mounted raids on Digarcha and plundered the assets of the monastery belonging to Panchen Lama, a ranking Tibetan spiritual leader. The incident, however, gave China an excellent opportunity to rise against Nepal. In a letter of admonishment, a Chinese general wrote: 'Nepal has committed a criminal offence by taking away the gifts belonging to the Panchen Lama. The entire loot should be promptly returned.' The matter came up for debate at the Courtiers' Council as to what action ought to be taken. In the end, it was decided that in the interest of Nepal, they should seek assistance from the British and that it was vital to conclude a pact with them.

This was precisely the opportunity that the British had been waiting for; they had long been desirous of entering Nepal not only to assess the obtaining situation but also to have a say in the internal affairs of the country. Generally speaking, the Nepalese courtiers had been unwilling to let any British officer into the Nepalese capital. At this difficult time, however, their position on the matter could not remain unchanged. Nepal was thus forced to conclude a trade treaty with the British, and as stipulated by the accord, Nepal gave a permit to Munsi Abdul Kaadir to visit the country as a representative of the British government. Heartened by the treaty, the British forced the King of Garhwal to cede his territory to Nepal; a letter from the Nawab of Abadh Pradesh to the Nawab of Rampur was used for the purpose. The Garhwalis, who were also passing through a difficult phase at this time, easily accepted Nepal's sovereignty. However, while the revolts raised by the Baise kings petered out gradually, Nepal's enmity with Tibet deepened further.

While Nepal was concluding the trade treaty with the British, Chinese General Tung-Thang, leading some nine thousand soldiers, had marched into the Nepalese territory via Kerung. Another Chinese battalion had entered Nepal via Kuti. While the Nepalese troops successfully held up the Chinese Army entering Nepal from the north-east at Listi, those entering Nepal from the north-west made a gradual advance towards the capital, Kathmandu. But here the Chinese Army ran into trouble, and began to discuss entering into a treaty with Nepal. After the Chinese proposed that it would be convenient for them to hold talks at Dhaibung, the Nepalese soldiers left it, retreating to their side of the Betravati River. The discussions dragged on for about one month as the two sides could not arrive at an agreement on the terms of reference. Then the Chinese stated that Dhaibung, too, lacked adequate facilities and that Nuwakot would be a better place to hold talks to thrash out the differences. This was clearly a ploy employed by the Chinese side to make its way towards Kathmandu; so the Nepalese Army made preparations to stop the Chinese from crossing the Betravati River.

At this, a Chinese commander leading some three thousand soldiers charged over the bridge at Betravati. The Nepalese soldiers stationed at Gerkhu and Chokde put up a tough fight and went on to defeat the Chinese troops. The Chinese accepted the defeat almost immediately. Then the Nepalese Army, even as the Chinese soldiers were fleeing from the bridge, proceeded to pull it down in order to forestall the possibility of the reinforcement of the Chinese troops. As the bridge collapsed, some one thousand Chinese soldiers fell into the river and drowned. This took place on 20 August 1792.

The morale of the Chinese Army was at a low following the Nepalese victory. Soon, winter set in, threatening the closure of the Himalayan passes and, consequently, the supply of food. All this forced the Chinese to again raise rather seriously the matter of the treaty. The Nepalese side agreed. At the end of the talks, the Nepalese side agreed to return all the property looted in Digarcha. On the demand of the Chinese, Nepal also agreed to relinquish the Kerung and Khasa areas to Tibet.

Shyamarpa was handed over to the Chinese on the condition that he would be exempted from any kind of punishment or punitive action. However, on the way back to Tibet, at his first night halt, Shyamarpa poisoned himself.

Prince Bahadur Shah had entered into the trade treaty with the British with the intent of buying arms for the war against the Chinese. But no arms were made available to Nepal, notwithstanding several entreaties. 'The British are real opportunists,' remarked an unhappy and irritated prince. By now Bahadur Shah had developed a dislike for the British from the core of his heart. However, because of their growing popularity and influence, he was unable to raise any protest directly.

In mid-1793, King Ranabahadur Shah turned eighteen. The Shah royal dynasty of Gorkha maintained a tradition under which a regent could represent the king in running the affairs of the state until the latter came of age and had to surrender the authority when the king attained adulthood. Accordingly, it was time for Bahadur Shah to hand over to the king all the authority concerning the administration of the kingdom. But he knew quite well that the king would not be able to run the administration efficiently. He also knew and feared that the failure to hand over power in time would lead to feud and acrimony in the family. So he prepared himself to fully hand over the powers to the king. But because of the war, all the administrative arrangements of the country had fallen into disarray, so the king was unwilling to assume all the responsibilities forthwith. A kind of joint rule by the uncle and nephew prevailed for about one year——with the views and opinion of the nephew prevailing over those of the uncle, in real terms.

Once King Ranabahadur took total control, Bahadur Shah was automatically overthrown. Thereafter, when the new Courtiers' Council was appointed on 26 June 1794, Rajrajeswori, the older consort of the king, was designated as the 'senior queen' and appointed as his principal adviser. His second wife, Subarnaprabha, the mother of Ranodyot Shah, was accorded the title of 'queen'. At this time, the position of chautara was perhaps the most coveted, so there were many aspirants to it. On the one hand, Balabhadra Shah laid claims to it, saying that he belonged to the high caste and was a close relation of the royal family; on the other, Bidur Shahi and Sherbahadur Shahi made similar claims, saying that they were as brothers to the king (by virtue of their being the offspring of the king's stepmother). Bom Shah was another aspirant to the position of chautara. Bahadur Shah made no claims for the position, having lost all hopes of getting it. Finally, the king accorded the position to the brothers Bidur Shahi and Sherbahadur Shahi, jointly. When the new council of ministers was formed, Tribhuvan Pradhan (Khawas) and Narsingh Gurung found a place in it, while Abhimansingh Basnyat and Damodar Pande were retained from the old Cabinet.

A huge celebration was held in Kathmandu to mark the king's assumption of powers and his taking control of the administration. Almost everything went well for about a year. But as time passed, King Ranabahadur turned out to be a carefree and indulgent individual. He spent his days pursuing the pleasures of life, secure in the belief that the administration was in the hands of experienced ministers who would leave no stone unturned to improve the overall situation of the country; he was convinced that the ministers would bring no harm to the nation.

Though handsome in appearance, Ranabahadur was said to have an unkind heart. He was fond of singing and playing the guitar. His penchant for music kept him away from valorous activities such as fighting or hunting. Indeed, he was scared of horse riding, and moved about alongisde humans. He enjoyed animal and bird fights, so the palace was home to various kinds of animals and birds. He evinced a special interest in bullfighting. For this purpose, he would bring big bulls from faraway places in neighbouring India. To keep the bulls, he had a wide pasture in Kathmandu (in the area presently occupied by the airport), which was manned by one *sandhevaidya* (literally, bull physician) and several attendants. Cottages were built to shelter the bulls and store fodder.

Around this time, Ranabahadur married a beauty from Tirhut in south Nepal. Her name was Kantabati. The king marrying a Brahmin widow left Bahadur Shah baffled and dumbfounded. In his eyes, a Brahmin widow being forced into wedlock by a member of the Shah royal family that had for generations venerated the cow and the Brahmin, was a reprehensible crime. However, fearful of the cruel disposition of his nephew, he did not protest. Actually, it was at this point of time that differences began to grow between the two, leading to an open feud. Then, as a bolt out of the blue, Bidur Shahi and Sherbahadur Shahi, moved over to the house inside the royal palace compound where Bahadur Shah himself had been residing. Despite his long tenure as the prime minister as well as the regent, Bahadur Shah had not bothered to make arrangements for a separate residence for himself, resting content with living in an ordinary building inside the palace compound. Whatever land he had inherited from his father, he had given it away to a *guthi* (trust), and had even constructed a small *dharmshala* (pilgrim's house) near the temple of Pashupatinath as shelter for visiting pilgrims. After Bidur and Sherbahadur moved into his house, a distressed and sorrowful Bahadur Shah left the palace compound and went over to the pilgrim's house of Pashupati as if he were a person without shelter.

Prince Bahadur Shah, who once was gallantly involved in the running of the affairs of the state, now became an outcast, forced to spend time with visiting pilgrims, mostly in debate and discourse on God and the afterlife. One can only imagine his plight and the pain of living an inert life, devoid of happiness and enjoyment. But whom could he share his feelings with? While the campaign to the west had been completed in one way, the people of those provinces had not fully accepted, at least sentimentally, Nepal's sovereignty over them, mainly due to shortcomings in how the administration was run. The nation's administrative system was crying out for comprehensive reforms. Bahadur Shah had foreseen the danger of betrayal by the British if the Nepalese administration failed to introduce timely reforms. But King Ranabahadur and his coterie of advisers seemed to be unaware of all this, indifferent and busy enjoying the carnal pleasures of life. Bahadur Shah was growing impatient, but he was also helpless.

After all, he had no option but to remain withdrawn from an active life, something he had never imagined would be his plight. Earlier, during his periodic exiles in India he had found out that the British had no positive outlook vis-à-vis Nepal. So this time he resolved not to go to India.

Meanwhile, King Ranabahadur had promised to Kantabati that her son would be his successor. He was so head over heels in love with Kantabati that he was eager to fulfil every wish or desire she expressed. Bahadur Shah viewed all this with disdain. The king, too, was aware that his uncle had only disdain and dislike for him; so he and his advisers were looking for pretexts to remove the obstacle that presented itself in the form of Bahadur Shah.

Around the middle of 1795, Bahadur Shah quietly wrote a letter to Sung-Yung, the Chinese resident agent also known as Amban, in Lhasa, Tibet, saying his nephew had taken all his powers from him and that he was relegated to living in a pilgrim's house, spending time in worship and prayers. Clearly, the letter was prompted by the hope of getting some kind of moral support from the Chinese kingdom. In his reply, the Chinese Amban advised that 'both the uncle and nephew should have cordial feelings for each other and should also work in unison'. The reply was addressed to Ranabahadur too, making a reference to Bahadur Shah's letter. For his part, the king stayed quiet, without reacting to the development in any way. The next year the Chinese emperor died and his son Chia-ch'ing ascended the throne, and Bahadur Shah again wrote to Sung, this time expressing his desire to visit China 'to pay respect to the new emperor'. The Nepalese prince's letter put the Chinese resident agent in a dilemma. He knew that the denial of permit for a visit aimed at paying respect to the new emperor, that too requested by a distinguished personage like Bahadur Shah, who had been honoured with the title of Ghung by the Chinese emperor, would be beyond civilized manners. But by this time, the Amban was well aware of the rift between Bahadur Shah and his nephew the king. So, without replying to the prince, he wrote a letter to Ranabahadur, aimed at knowing exactly why his uncle wanted to visit China, and what the king's opinion would be in this regard.

The letter said:

Do you (Wang) know or don't know that 'Ghung' Bahadur Shah has written to us expressing his desire to visit China? He is your uncle, yet one of your nobles, so it may not be possible to receive him in China without your consent. If you think he could be sent to have an audience with the Emperor, advise us accordingly. While notifying us in this regard, your uncle should be asked whether he intends to return or settle here, after meeting the Emperor. It is important that we know about this. If it is not important to send him here, a prompt reply to this letter may be unnecessary . . .

Actually, Bahadur Shah had committed no serious crime by expressing his intent to visit China. But Ranabahadur became furious and he sent his soldiers to arrest Bahadur Shah, and cast him into prison on the night of 19 February 1797. A summons was also served asking the prince to present himself at the royal palace to explain the cause that had led him to write the letter to the Chinese Amban. But the prince, familiar as he was with the hostile nature of his nephew, declined to present himself before the king, and instead sent a letter:

> . . . You should do whatever suits you. To ignore the royal call is indeed undesirable. Haven't felt uncomfortable staying here [in prison], but don't feel comfortable to come over there. You have absolutely no sympathy for me. So it is better for me to stay out here . . .

Bahadur Shah's decision not to present himself at the royal palace infuriated the king further. The letter had also mentioned the king's cruel disposition and the uncle's regret over it. A reply to the letter by the Chinese Amban was yet to be delivered. It was now decided that Bahadur Shah had to be crushed, once and for all. So Sarbajit Pande, Chamu Bhandari and Ajit Khadka were sent to Lhasa to intimate the Amban about all the charges served against Bahadur Shah.

The following were some of the charges levelled against the uncle by the nephew:

- In connivance with Dalmardan Shah, Bahadur Shah had plotted to put to death Ranabahadur's father, King Pratapsingh Shah, and throw his torso out of a window.
- Bahadur Shah had had Sarbajit Rana beheaded after falsely accusing him of having an illicit relationship with Queen Mother Rajendralaxmi.
- Bahadur Shah had planned to kill Ranabahadur and then bury his body in the well of Dakhchowk.

- He had made an attempt on the life of Queen Mother Rajendralaxmi by poisoning her, with the help of maid Mathura.
- During the night halt at Borlangghat, while Bahadur Shah was on his way to Gorkha for his wedding, he had planned to kill Ranabahadur and then throw the body into the river Gandaki.
- Bahadur Shah had scolded Bandhu Rana for allowing Ranabahadur to get out of the house.
- Due to the evil spirit invoked by Bahadur Shah in order to put the king to death, Ranabahadur, while returning after paying homage to Dakshinkali, had suffered from diarrhoea, and vomited thrice.
- When Bahadur Shah came looking for the king at midnight, he was attacked by one of the dogs guarding the palace and then he killed it 'for nothing'.
- Bahadur Shah had made reckless use of the royal seal during the king's absence.
- With the intent of killing Ranabahadur, Bahadur Shah had visited the king's place at midnight, but an attendant, Puni, having got wind of the matter, bolted the doors from inside. An angry Bahadur Shah went back, but only after slashing the doors with his sword.
- Bahadur Shah had perpetually ignored the 'Three Salutes', a way of paying respect to the monarch.
- Bahadur Shah had 'nearly sunk' the country by waging an 'unnecessary' war with Tibet, thereby 'undermining the cordial ties' that existed between the two countries dating to the time of King Ram Shah.

- His intention behind extending the hand of friendship towards the British had been to wage war with Tibet.

There was an old fort, built long ago during the times of the Malla kings, in the south-west corner of Kathmandu city, a little below Bhimsensthan. The Gorkhalis had been making use of this fort sometimes as a guest house and sometimes as a jail. Prince Bahadur Shah was detained at this fort for about four months. Ranabahadur had initiated all these suppressive moves against his uncle, as advised by his hard-line followers such as Bidur Shahi and Sherbahadur Shahi.

At this fort, on the Saturday night of 24 June 1797, Bahadur Shah was clandestinely put to death, possibly hanged. But it was given out that he had died a natural death. His mortal remains were cremated at Pashupati Aryaghat the very next day. Had there been no foul play, there was no reason why his body should have been so speedily cremated. There can be no doubt that he was murdered, given that the charges against him were fabricated ones.

Thus, an able builder of Nepal met his tragic end at the prime age of about thirty-eight, bringing about an abrupt halt to the all-important campaign of the unification of the Nepalese kingdom. Unattended was the task of administrative reforms in the provinces that had been won over; the military was in a state of disarray; and the routes and passes were worn out. As a consequence, the Nepalese would later suffer defeat at the hands of the British. Parts of Nepal's extended territories too were lost for good. As for Bahadur Shah's widow, little or almost nothing is known about her fate.

The king was happy about his uncle's departure; he could not foresee the difficulties that would crop up in the wake of Bahadur Shah's death. Bidur and Sherbahadur, too, were delighted as they could now easily climb the ladder of power. But old-time nobles and courtiers like Balabhadra Shah and Srikrishna Shah felt sad and anguished; they were also worried about their own fate. They thus started making preparations to flee the country, exercising utmost discretion.

Following the murder of Bahadur Shah, terror spread in the governing circles of Nepal. A series of murders and conspiracies were set off at the royal palace, while the general populace felt various calamities being thrust upon it. No courtier or noble dared to speak out against the prince's murder for fear of reprisal from Ranabahadur as well as from Bidur and Sherbahadur. Even though the courtiers and nobles harboured deep respect for Bahadur Shah, they called him a 'devil' in public.

Bahadur Shah has indeed a pride of place in the hearts of all nationalistic and patriotic Nepalese who will continue to remember him as an able son of an equally able father—King Prithvinarayan Shah, the builder of modern Nepal. Prince Bahadur Shah was his real successor.

Unpublished, written around 1961

Two

The Beheading of Damodar Pande

Animosity characterized the relationship between King Ranabahadur Shah's two wives, the senior queen, Rajrajeswori, and the second wife, Subarnaprabha. While Rajrajeswori had borne only one daughter from Ranabahadur, Subarnaprabha had mothered two sons. And the latter had vowed that her eldest son, Ranodyot Shah, would succeed his father to the throne. Small wonder then that Rajrajeswori harboured some jealousy towards Subarnaprabha.

In the year 1796, Ranabahadur met a young Brahmin widow named Kantabati who hailed from Mithila—he probably first set eyes on her at Pashupati, the holy Hindu shrine, where Kantabati was on a pilgrimage on the occasion of Shivaratri. The king fell head over heels in love with the widow's youthful beauty and charm. And acting on the advice of his brothers Bidur Shahi and Sherbahadur Shahi, he had Kantabati arrested; she was forcibly carried in a box and taken to the royal palace. The Brahmin girl, however, was dismayed at her plight. The social custom and practice of the time prohibited remarriage for widows; moreover, in those days, a relationship between a

Brahmin female and a Kshatriya male was considered abnormal and therefore condemnable. So she was reluctant to marry Ranabahadur even though he was the king. No less stunned were her patrons who had accompanied her to Pashupati. Kantabati stuck to her stance for about six months, rejecting the monarch's marriage proposal, but buckled after the king conveyed through Rajrajeswori that Kantabati 'should have no doubt' that the son borne by her would inherit the throne.

As was to be expected, Subarnaprabha was opposed to this marriage; so too were several elderly courtiers. Rajrajeswori, however, felt that it would be better if the right to succession went to the offspring of Kantabati rather than to Subarnaprabha's son; so she favoured the marriage. Accordingly, the king tied the nuptial knot with Kantabati at the royal palace in Gorkha sometime in the second half of the year 1796.

On 2 October 1797, Queen Kantabati gave birth to Prince Girbanyuddha. As promised by the king, he was duly declared the heir apparent. Until this time, the Shah dynasty of Gorkha had taken itself as belonging to the Somabamsi-Kshatriya clan, but now, for an unexplained reason, it accepted the Parmaar dynasty of Ujjain of India as its ancestry, borrowing the title of Bikram to be added to the baby prince's name. So he came to be known as Girbanyuddhabikram Shah. Thus began the tradition of all the male members of the Nepalese royal family carrying the title Bikram in their names.

Less than a year after Girban's birth, Kantabati suddenly took ill, bringing great agony and distress to Ranabahadur. As her condition deteriorated, the queen began worrying about whether her son would actually get to succeed to the throne. Noticing the queen's impatience, some sycophantic nobles and courtiers began filling her ears, saying that the king would likely abdicate the throne immediately if adequate pressure was put on him. On the other hand, Regent Rajrajeswori thought that her very survival would be at stake if the crown, perchance, went to the son of Subarnaprabha. So she too favoured the immediate handing over of the throne to Girban.

Kantabati had fallen victim to tuberculosis, then an incurable ailment, so no physician had come forward to treat her. But the king had some kind of faith and trust in Laxminarayan Dahal, a vet who, because he specialized in treating bulls, was known as sandhevaidya, and appointed him as the first physician to take care of the queen (before him, nobody had been appointed as physician to treat Kantabati). In the beginning, Dahal assured the king that Kantabati would recover, saying that 'the evil spirits of the devil Bahadur Shah were troubling the queen; I will drive away the spirits by invoking my god, and she will be all right.' Unfortunately, the god he invoked never materialized and the queen's health showed no improvement. Around this time, Kirtimansingh Basnyat, who had once been dismissed from the service of the royal court, became one of Ranabahadur's close advisers. Basnyat, by way of a special entreaty and promises of rewards, got another vet, Milham Vaidya, to try his hand at treating the queen. The vaidya urged both the king and queen to wear saffron robes, saying that it was 'important to have control over the genitals for treatment of this disease'. Kirtimansingh concurred with the physician's proposition and accordingly advised the king:

'Your Majesty should retire to the *banaprastha* [the third stage in the *barnasrama* system wherein a person retires to a forest life]. Let's place Girban on the throne. You will not incur any loss—the queen, too, harbours such a desire, and this will give her some peace of mind.' Gajaraj Mishra, the royal preceptor, vehemently opposed the plan of the king's abdication, but he was deported. Another opponent to the plan, Srikrishna Shah, the son of Mahoddamkirti Shah, was forced to flee the country. The king remained in a dilemma for a couple of months. While it was enormously difficult for him to let his beloved queen down, no less painful was the prospect of prematurely handing over the crown.

Subsequently, as planned by Kirtimansingh Basnyat, the Courtiers' Council sat for a high-level meeting. Some one hundred nobles and courtiers attending the meeting vowed through a dharmapatra that if Prince Girban were given the throne, they would 'serve the nation and the king with doubled devotion and loyalty'. Ranabahadur was pleased with the courtiers' pledge; thus, deriving strength from the trust document, the one-and-a-half-year-old Girban was crowned the King of Nepal. It was Prithvipal Sen, the King of the Palpa province, who placed the crown on the head of the infant king, on 8 March 1798. Rajrajeswori was also retained in her position as the minor king's patron.

Unmindful of the harsh reality that the crown once taken off his head would never come back, Ranabahadur was committing a blunder. He had thought and hoped that even after relinquishing the crown, the nobles and courtiers would continue to hold him in high regard and that his orders would be carried out as usual. He was grossly unaware that all this would amount to hoping against hope.

Under the Nepalese monarchic tradition, an ex-king was not allowed to stay in the state capital after a new king had been crowned. Accordingly, the twenty-three-year-old Ranabahadur declared that he 'had enjoyed the pleasures of running the state, as allotted to him by destiny'; that he was renouncing worldly ties as he desired to spend time in meditation; and that he was voluntarily giving up state authority. Donning saffron robes and giving himself the new name of Swami Nirgunananda, he moved over to Devpatan near the Pashupati temple, accompanied by his wife Kantabati who, too, had become an ascetic, though ailing. However, despite Ranabahadur's renunciation, his interest in watching the bullfights that occasionally took place at the nearby pasture of Thulo Gaucharan did not diminish.

Meanwhile, as the patron of the minor king, Rajrajeswori chose to stay at the royal palace. Ranabahadur's sons from Subarnaprabha, the four-year-old Ranodyot Shah and his younger brother, Shumsher Shah (age not known), were appointed ministers. So, acting as their representative, the second queen, too, stayed at the palace. Ranabahadur's brothers Bidur and Sherbahadur also carried on with their duties at the royal palace as senior state officials.

By this time, Kantabati's condition was growing worse by the day. She was receiving treatment at the sanatorium of Devpatan, with the physicians Laxminarayan and Milham doing their utmost. Although Milham was a competent and qualified medical practitioner of the time, all his efforts to cure the queen were in vain as at the time it was impossible to cure anybody of tuberculosis. Milham would often say: 'I will drive away the evil spirits bedevilling the queen by invoking God.' But as often, he would also say: 'God is reluctant. He wouldn't listen.' The queen rapidly lost her health, and this surely added to the woes and grief of Ranabahadur. Finding that both the physicians were failing to cure his wife, the former king not only became furious but also started to act with vengeance. One of Milham's hands was crushed at an oil crushing plant. And a Brahmin that he was, Laxminarayan was forcibly fed food that his caste didn't allow him to consume; his head was tonsured, while his eyes were filled with the milk drops of *siundi* (cactus) before he was shunted out of the border in the south. His wife was handed over to a low-caste *damai* (tailor). Milham died of pain from his crushed hand. The houses of both the physicians were set on fire and all their property was confiscated.

Overwhelmed by grief, Ranabahadur thereafter moved from Devpatan to Pulchowk in Patan, along with Kantabati. As the condition of the queen's health continued to grow worse, and as no benefit was being obtained from treatment, attempts were made to cure the queen by offering prayers to different deities. Tantric rituals as well as *yagnya*, the ceremony of sacrifice, were performed. Brahmin and Buddhist priests performed prayers and other rituals at different religious centres; money and other offerings, too, flowed profusely. Land and property were given away in abundance. Meanwhile, when word spread that a vulture had descended on the roof of the royal palace—an ill omen—orders were issued nationwide to slaughter all the country's vultures. Despite all these efforts however, there was no regaining the health of the queen, who was finally taken to the Pashupati Aryaghat on 1 November 1799 where she died that very day.

Heartbroken at the loss of Kantabati, Ranabahadur lamented: 'My living in this world is meaningless; I will die jumping into the funeral pyre of the queen.' However, after a good deal of persuasion, he was taken back to Pulchowk. Rajrajeswori now found herself in a tight spot. She could not abandon Ranabahadur who had now become mentally unstable. Nor could she leave the infant king at the royal palace to fend for himself. Ranabahadur could also not be called back to the palace after he had become a recluse, choosing to live the banaprastha way of life. So, Rajrajeswori would oversee the conduct of the daily administrative work of the court during the day, and head for Pulchowk to spend the night with Ranabahadur.

After Kantabati's passing away, Ranabahadur became embittered with the deities who had been invoked and worshipped in the hope that his wife would recover her health. As an act of revenge, he resolved to defy and deface those gods and goddesses. The Buddhist priests and Brahmins who had on his behalf offered prayers at temples and monasteries, and who had been rewarded with money and other donations, too became the objects of Ranabahadur's wrath. In the process, the idols and images of the various deities of the Kathmandu valley were defiled and desecrated. Ranabahadur even set himself to blasting the Pashupati temple with cannon fire, but was somehow dissuaded from the act. On his orders, the image of Tulaja-Bhawani was dug up from her shrine and thrown to the cremation ground. An axe was used to pound and smash the statue of Betal (the symbol of tantric spirits) located in Bhadgaon, while the Haratimaata of Swayambhu was offered incense made of human excreta, and then her idol dug up and thrown into the nearby jungle. The Shivalinga (the phallus symbol of Lord Shiva) of Kumbheswor was smeared with human excreta, and many other deities, too, met a similar fate. Money and other donations were forcibly recovered from the Brahmin and Buddhist priests even as they were subjected to abuses and invectives.

Thereafter, Ranabahadur shed the look of an ascetic and, in clear violation of the terms of the trust document, began to directly interfere in the affairs of the state, making life difficult for the courtiers who had sworn their allegiance to the minor King Girban. Intolerant of such acts of interference, the courtiers not only became wary of the ex-king and his followers but also began devising ways of dealing with the unwelcome situation.

So Kirtimansingh Basnyat made arrangements under which King Girban was taken away from the capital to the royal palace at Nuwakot under the pretext of observing the annual Fagu festival of colours. This was on 20 January 1800. Rajrajeswori, the regent, was in a tight spot once again. While she could not abandon the almost-senile Ranabahadur in Kathmandu, she could not also risk leaving the minor King Girban alone in Nuwakot. So she began visiting Nuwakot once every eight to ten days to affix the royal seal on the documents issued under the name of the king; the rest of the time she stayed with

Ranabahadur at Pulchowk. Ranabahadur did not like the queen dividing her time thus, nor were the likes of Kirtimansingh happy or satisfied. If anything, she earned only disapproval from either side.

Once, Ranabahadur went over to the Nuwakot durbar. Greatly annoyed and furious with the nobles and courtiers for what he thought was the abduction of the infant king from Kathmandu, he ordered a series of punishments. He got some of the nobles and courtiers hung on the walls, with their hands tied. For no known offence, Sirdar Amarsingh Thapa and Ranabom Pande were hung, with their feet tied; Parasuram Thapa was placed on a piece of hide and dragged to the marketplace; while Prabal Rana was forced to wear his wife's clothes and paraded in the marketplace. All this was viewed with disdain by Rajrajeswori who finally managed to persuade Ranabahadur to return to Pulchowk.

Meanwhile, as the violent acts of the ex-king had rendered the task of running the administration difficult, the nobles and courtiers loyal to King Girban came up with a plan to intern Ranabahadur along with Rajrajeswori who had all along stood by his side. Almost all the nobles and courtiers of Nuwakot arrived at the consensus that Ranabahadur should be held under house arrest if only to be administered treatment. They knew only too well that if they failed to do so, they would become victims of Ranabahadur's vengeful acts. Balabhadra Shah, however, disagreed with this plan of action and, fleeing Nuwakot by night, he reached Pulchowk to inform the ex-king and Rajrajeswori about the details of the plan of the Nuwakot courtiers, including Kirtimansingh's. At this, both became livid and, heedless of the consequences, declared that they had reassumed the authority of the state. They dissolved the Nuwakot-based Courtiers' Council, and appointed a new council—though illegal—at Pulchowk. When the new council was formed, the post of senior minister naturally went to Balabhadra Shah, while Bidur Shahi was appointed the second minister in charge. Pran Shah succeeded in getting the position of the third minister. The other members of the council were Pratiman Rana, Ranakeshar Pande, Jaharsingh Basnyat and Amarsingh Thapa (Junior)—father of Bhimsen Thapa.

With the installation of a new house of nobility at Pulchowk, a kind of dual rule came to be introduced in Nepal. On the one hand, Ranabahadur and Rajrajeswori exercised their control over the Kathmandu valley, while on the other, the lawful King Girban and his nobles and courtiers governed the rest of the kingdom from Nuwakot where Queen Subarnaprabha, too, resided with her sons. While most of the nobles and courtiers at the Nuwakot durbar were loyal to Girban, a small number had shifted their loyalty to the camp of Ranabahadur. In the meantime, the Pulchowk-based courtiers started creating a front against the legitimate administration of Nuwakot. The army personnel and officers of the Taradal, Ranasher, Ranabhim and Devidutta regiments who were stationed in Kathmandu moved to Ranabahadur's side, while most of the remaining military units along with their officers remained loyal to King Girban. Each side was also making frantic appeals to the army and people across the country in order to elicit support. From Kathmandu, messages were being sent speedily on behalf of Ranabahadur, saying, 'Immediately report here to help me'; while letters bearing the official seal of King Girban were being sent out from the Nuwakot palace with calls 'to report here immediately without entering the Char Bhanjyang [Kathmandu valley]' so as to 'continue giving assistance to me as provided by the trust document'.

King Girban also made a call to the people of Patan: 'Attempts are afoot from the evil elements to violate the trust document, to drive a wedge in the relationship between me and my father, and to wage a war between us; we hear that, instigated by these elements, you, too, are prepared to fight; all of you are my subjects, just as those who are here with me; Swamiji [Ranabahadur] is my father and I am his son; under whose orders are you ready to fight?'

On the other side, Rajrajeswori sent out messages, saying: 'Should you think good and well of Swamiji, come to us immediately; but if you are loyal to the evil elements of Nuwakot, you should be prepared to fight.'

In this war of words or of getting the message across to the people, the Nuwakot government had an upper hand as it had control over the most potent means of communication of the time: the *hulak* (the post). While the messages sent out on behalf of Ranabahadur failed to reach their destinations on time, those given out by the Nuwakot palace were delivered regularly and on time, with the result that in due course, all the army personnel stationed at the administrative centres of the west reported to the Nuwakot palace.

Following this, under the directive of Kirtimansingh,

an army battalion led by Damodar Pande left Nuwakot for the Kathmandu valley. En route, the brigade successfully won over Ranabahadur's garrison at Kakani and, advancing further towards the capital, arrived at Mudkhu. Hearing that the Nuwakot Army was arriving in Kathmandu shortly, Ranabahadur and his associates panicked and decided to run away. Leaving Rajrajeswori behind, Ranabahadur fled Pulchowk on the night of 10 May 1800 and, passing through Chapagaon, Piutar and finally the pass of Parsa, entered India to lead a retired life in Benaras.

Close on the heels of Ranabahadur, on the third day of his departure, Rajrajeswori, too, left for Benaras, accompanied by a few women attendants. Balabhadra was also with the queen. Kirtimansingh and Damodar Pande did not try to stop them from leaving. On the very day that Rajrajeswori left for Benaras, King Girban was brought to Kathmandu from Nuwakot. With the departure of both Ranabahadur and the queen, the Courtiers' Council appointed by them in Kathmandu stood automatically dissolved, while the old council that had shifted over to Nuwakot was revived. There was one difference, however: Queen Subarnaprabha became the regent and patron of the minor princes. Kirtimansingh was retained as prime minister, while Damodar Pande served as minister. Sirdar Amarsingh Thapa (Senior) was conferred the title of *kazi* (minister) and inducted into the Courtiers' Council.

On the other side, Ranabahadur and his associates, who had now arrived in Benaras, were most furious with Damodar as they believed that it was he who had led the assault on Kathmandu from Nuwakot.

In Benaras, the British played good hosts to Ranabahadur. Bhimsen Thapa, the ex-king's bodyguard, who too had fled with Ranabahadur, and Ranganath Pandit, the son of Brajanath Pandit, were assigned as his principal advisers; Bhimsen Thapa had already managed to obtain the title of Sirdar from the ex-king. Also available to serve Ranabahadur were a few nobles, all of whom had earlier been removed from their positions in Nepal: Pran Shah, Hastadal Shah, Purna Shah, Kazi Birbhadra Shah, Dalbhanjan Pande and Balnarsingh Kunwar. Some young men like Bhairab Singh and Udaya Giri also became active as Ranabahadur's assistants. All Ranabahadur's associates now planned to respectfully get their king back to Nepal as soon as possible and in whatever way possible, with the aid of the British East India Company.

As for the British, they had for long been awaiting the opportunity to interfere in the internal affairs of Nepal; now they were ready to take advantage of the feuding that was taking place within the Nepalese monarchy. When Bhimsen Thapa and his associates requested the British to help them to get Ranabahadur back to Kathmandu, they acted as if they were turning a deaf ear to them, but at the same time they (the British) took the opportunity to sound out their interest in concluding a commerce treaty with the Nepalese kingdom. A proposal in this regard was sent to Kathmandu through Brajanath Pandit, who had been staying in Benaras at that time. On their part, Kirtimansingh and other courtiers were at first hesitant, but later showed their readiness to enter into the treaty on the condition that Ranabahadur would remain in Benaras. Accordingly, Pandit Gajaraj Mishra who represented the Nepalese administration and a British officer representing the East India Company began to hold discussions in Patna on the provisions of the treaty. Right at that moment, however, a tragic incident took place in Kathmandu.

Rajrajeswori's men had been spreading rumours that Kazi Kirtimansingh and Queen Subarnaprabha were involved in an illicit relationship. On the night of 28 September 1801, at around nine, two assailants murdered Kirtimansingh while he was returning to his residence from the palace after holding consultations with Sherbahadur Shahi. Kirtimansingh's body was found in a room in a house in Hattisaar the next day. The assailants had fled but were identified, and an extensive search was also under way to identify the person who had given the orders for the assassination. Consequently, some eighty courtiers and officers belonging to the camp of Rajrajeswori were detained. Damoder Pande was one among those arrested, but was set free after he clutched his *janai* (sacred thread) and swore: 'I have committed no crime. I will not run away under any circumstances. I will accept punishment if proven guilty.' Bidur Shahi fled the scene, aided by brother Sherbahadur Shahi, who asked Bidur to go to a room downstairs for further inquiry into the allegation. Damodar's son Ranakeshar Pande as well as many other nobles and courtiers were put in chains. Ranajit Pande, father-in-law of one of Bhimsen Thapa's brothers, took to his heels, dashing off to Madhesh. Some nobles and courtiers were accused of both spreading the 'vicious rumours' and of being the accomplices in the murder. Some five to seven courtiers were beheaded on these charges, while Devdutta Thapa had his eyes gouged out.

The actual killers, however, were at large.

Following the murder of Kirtimansingh, his brother Bakhtabarsingh Basnyat was appointed the chief kazi and prime minister, while Damodar Pande and Amarsingh Thapa (Senior) continued to be members of the council of ministers. Subuddhi Khadka was appointed the principal adviser to the queen. Meanwhile, in Patna, the drafts of the proposed treaty between the East India Company government and the Nepalese administration were drawn up. The treaty enjoined the Nepalese administration to grant Ranabahadur an annual allowance of Nepalese rupees 80,000 and some property in kind out of the income derived from Pallo Kiraant and Vijayapur. In return, Ranabahadur would refrain from interfering in any way in Nepal's internal affairs. And should he be staying in India, he had to remain under the observation of the British government. Under the treaty provision, Ranabahadur could enter Nepal, but would be under the watchful eye of the Nepalese state. The treaty also asked of the Nepalese state to permit a British envoy to live as a Resident in Nepal, besides allowing the East India Company to open a trade mart in the Nepalese capital. The treaty had several provisions that aimed at benefiting the British greatly, while subjecting Nepal to some kind of domination.

The British envoy, Captain Knox, accompanied by Pandit Gajaraj Mishra, left for Nepal, carrying the draft proposal of the treaty. After some simple discussions, the treaty was ratified. Subsequently, Subarnaprabha sent Damodar Pande down to the Terai to receive Knox, who, accompanied by some of his assistants, arrived in Kathmandu on 18 April 1802 in order to carry out his duties there as the British envoy to Nepal.

Meanwhile, Ranabahadur was leading a royal life in Benaras in the glittering company of young women. He was apparently squandering all his resources; he was also frittering away Rajrajeswori's riches and jewellery. And as the resources waned, the couple began fighting. When Rajrajeswori found it difficult to stay with her husband any more in Benaras, she returned to Kathmandu, accompanied by Balabhadra and her women attendants. For a few days, she took shelter with the exiled king Harkumardutta Sen, at Ramnagar in Bettiah. Then she moved on towards Kathmandu—it was while she was staying at Rautahat that Kirtimansingh was slain in the Nepalese capital.

On hearing that Rajrajeswori had entered Nepal, Queen Subarnaprabha sent an army unit carrying an official letter asking the senior queen to return to Benaras, failing which, harsh measures would be taken against her. But the army contingent, unable to push the queen back from Rautahat, allowed her to stay put there. In the meantime, Balabhadra, Rajrajeswori's long-time loyalist and supporter, suddenly died, leaving her with only one option: returning to Kathmandu. But to stop her from returning, Subarnaprabha sent out a second army contingent; however, that too proved ineffective in checkmating her advance. Finding that Rajrajeswori and her women attendants were ready to draw their swords and fight in self-defence, the army officers did not dare arrest them; only the queen's other servants and load-carriers were rounded up. Then the queen and her attendants marched towards Kathmandu on foot. A third contingent of troops was sent from Kathmandu to halt them. Some officers of the unit sought to arrest the queen at Kulekhani, but the soldiers talked their officers out of it; instead, the queen and her entourage were welcomed, in a show of respect and loyalty. Carrying the queen in a palanquin on their shoulders, the soldiers brought her to Kimdole at Thankot on 27 November 1802. As it was not considered proper to go to the royal palace directly, Rajrajeswori stayed at Kimdole for a few days until some nobles and courtiers from the palace came to receive her.

Following these developments, Subarnaprabha suddenly grew edgy. She put on saffron robes and declared that she was leaving for Benaras. Then she left the palace for the precincts of the Pashupati temple where she starting living. Now the courtiers were left with no choice but to invite Rajrajeswori to the royal palace. So, Sherbahadur Shahi, Bakhtabarsingh, Damodar Pande and others organized a *sindoorjatra* (vermilion festival) to greet the senior queen into the palace. She was then made the regent and patron of the monarch. On her part, Rajrajeswori chose to forget the bitterness and animosities of the past; she called Subarnaprabha back to the palace, saying, 'Both of us sisters should stay together like before.' Accordingly, they started living together happily. And those ministers who had earlier been ousted were reinstated.

Now Rajrajeswori wanted to bring Ranabahadur back to Kathmandu even if it meant 'interning him here respectfully, if need be'. She made her wish known to the British and also sent messages asking for his release from Benaras. As for Ranabahadur himself, he was in a dire situation. Since no allowance had been sent to him by the Nepalese kingdom for the last two years, Ranabahadur had taken considerable amount of loans locally. From Seth Dwarakadas alone, he had borrowed 60,000 rupees. Knowing that the British would not set Ranabahadur free until all his loans were paid back, the queen made arrangements through Subba Hastadal Shah to pay back all the borrowed money.

When Rajrajeswori regained control of power, eight months had passed since the arrival of the British envoy Knox. The queen as well as many of her nobles and courtiers were none too happy with the presence of Captain Knox in Kathmandu, and were therefore looking for any opportunity to send him back. Exactly at this time, differences arose between Rajrajeswori and Subarnaprabha. And Captain Knox, who was aware of the elder queen's as well as her men's annoyance with his presence in Kathmandu and their plan to get him out, started dabbling in the politics of the kingdom, taking the side of Subarnaprabha. Rajrajeswori got wind of this matter and she dissolved the council of ministers. She then formed a new Courtier's Council on 18 July 1803. Bidur Shahi, a cousin of Ranabahadur, was promoted to the position of principal chautara, while Damodar Pande was elevated to the post of chief kazi and prime minister. As for Bakhtabarsingh, Balabanta Rana and Narsingh Gurung, they were retained as ministers.

On the day of the formation of the new council, Subarnaprabha and Bom Shah were imprisoned. Ten days later, ex-premier Bakhtabarsingh, too, was detained. Then envoy Knox had to leave after he was served with a notice asking him to move to Makawanpur. The notice read: 'Cholera has spread in Kathmandu; it is no longer safe to live here.'

From the documents of the time, no explanations can be found as to why Subarnaprabha, Bom Shah and Bakhtabarsingh Basnyat were arrested and why Knox was driven out of Kathmandu—acts that took place almost simultaneously. Yet there are suggestions to the effect that the arrests were triggered by the attempts that had supposedly been made to depose Rajrajeswori so as to hand power over to Subarnaprabha. At that time, secret agents like Pandit Padmapani, who had been sent to Kathmandu from Benaras by Bhimsen Thapa, had spread rumours in the capital of such a conspiracy.

As regards the insult, if any, that had been caused to the British through the driving away of Captain Knox from Kathmandu, the British were forced to swallow it as they were at that time engaged in a fierce war with the Marathas. However, the British were furious that Damodar Pande had been appointed the chief kazi. Envoy Knox was dead certain that it was Pande who had been instrumental in removing him from Kathmandu.

In due course, the British won the war with the Marathas and their authority in Delhi too was consolidated. Captain Knox was then called back from Makawanpur to India by Governor General Wellesley in a clear violation of the treaty that Britain had concluded with the Nepalese kingdom. The violation, however, came as a windfall to Ranabahadur, as it automatically rid him of British surveillance.

When the new Courtiers' Council had been appointed in Kathmandu, Bidur Shahi had become the senior minister. His brother Sherbahadur, however, had been removed from his ministerial position. So, Sherbahadur first fled to Nuwakot and then went over to Benaras to take the shelter provided by Ranabahadur. By this time, Ranabahadur had become a puppet in the hands of the likes of Bhimsen Thapa. Apart from Bhimsen, the other fugitive courtiers from Nepal who formed a clique with Ranabahadur in Benaras were: Pandit Ranganath Poudel, Dalbhanjan Pande, Ranadhoj Thapa and Udaya Giri. All of them were relatively immature and below the age of thirty. Bhimsen's plan was to wrest administrative control of Nepal from the hands of Rajrajeswori and Damodar Pande. Towards this end, he instigated Ranabahadur with the help and consent of his primarily young assistants. In a bid to support this plan, letters purportedly written by Ranabahadur were sent to many nobles and courtiers in Kathmandu.

According to the plan, Nepal's present council of ministers was to be dissolved, and a new council formed, with Bhimsen Thapa as the prime minister, Ranganath Poudel as the *rajguru* (royal preceptor), Sherbahadur Shahi as the seniormost minister and Dalbhanjan Pande as the senior minister. Ministerial positions were also in the offing for men like Ranajit Pande, Tribhuvan Pradhan (Khawas) and Amarsingh Thapa—all of whom had earlier been removed from their posts in Nepal.

But the execution of the plan was going to be difficult. Firstly, it involved money. Rajrajeswori had sent only as much money as would be needed for Ranabahadur's return to Kathmandu. At this, on his own initiative, Ranganath Poudel took a loan of Rs 40,000 from a business house upon a pledge by one of his acquaintances. As this would take care of the expenses of the way, preparations were made for a grand return home of Ranabahadur.

Informed about the plan conceived in Benaras, it was important for the authorities in Kathmandu to come up with a counter-plan. On 11 February 1804, three of Ranabahadur's favourite kazis—Tribhuvan Pradhan, Ranajit Pande and Amarsingh Thapa—as well as two or three sirdars, also said to belong to the ex-king's camp, were arrested and interned. Those in charge in Kathmandu decided that while Ranabahadur and his men would be allowed to return to the capital unhindered and a red carpet would be rolled out to welcome them, Ranabahadur for one would thereafter be held under strict observation. Damodar Pande and other courtiers knew quite well that taking the initiative to welcome Ranabahadur to Kathmandu would be a risky proposition; but to confront him would not be wise either. So, Damodar decided to take the risk of receiving Ranabahadur with open arms.

Damodar was physically stout, but his nature was less sturdy—he was a simple-minded, kind-hearted man, loyal to the country and the crown, and belonged to an illustrious family. Had he been one possessed of a brutal mind, he could have decimated all the nobles and courtiers who, after all, had been arrested and jailed on fictitious charges. He could also have taken under his control all the courtiers and assistants who had accompanied Ranabahadur from Benaras, and firmly dealt with the ex-king himself. But at this time, any such despicable act was unthinkable for Damodar, who most faithfully followed the dictum of Prithvinarayan Shah: 'Never ever kill your own brothers or courtiers.'

When Ranabahadur departed from Benaras for home, the Nepalese kingdom sent Narsingh Gurung along with an army brigade to escort him up to Kathmandu. Discussions had been held on where to keep Ranabahadur in Kathmandu, but no decision had been made yet. The prevailing norm prohibited Ranabahadur, who had once turned himself into a hermit, from entering the capital city directly; so, for the day he arrived, he was to be kept at Tundikhel, which was outside the city, near the temple of Lumadhi (Bhadrakali). Accordingly, tents and marquees were set up at Tundikhel, and special clothes and offerings to be presented to the Lumadhi-Bhagawati on behalf of Swamiji were arranged. However, neither Rajrajeswori nor Damodar, who had remained unflinchingly loyal to both the queen and the minor king, had any idea about what would transpire once Ranabahadur arrived in Kathmandu.

Meanwhile, Bhimsen Thapa and his aides had already won Narsingh over to their side. When Ranabahadur had asked for permission to return to Kathmandu, the British governor general not only gave him the papers, but also sent some military police up to Nepal's border in order to provide security for Ranabahadur. As this was enough of an indication of the fact that Swamiji had received support from the British government, Narsingh thought that he would be better off by switching loyalties.

So Narsingh, who was actually sent to keep watch on Ranabahadur while he returned, had now turned into the ex-king's bodyguard. Under his protection, Ranabahadur and his entourage advanced towards Kathmandu. According to the travel plan, he was scheduled to arrive at Thankot on

1 March 1804. Damodar and his associates waited at Thankot to receive the ex-king. An elephant too awaited Ranabahadur who was to ride on it to the palace; there were also soldiers at hand to honour him with a military salute.

No need was felt for the king to be present to welcome an ex-king, while Regent Rajrajeswori too chose to stay back at the royal palace. As Ranabahadur surfaced at the base of the Thankot Pass, he was accompanied by Sherbahadur Shahi and Bhimsen Thapa, among others. Seeing Narsingh, who was sent out for observation, acting as the bodyguard of Ranabahadur, Damodar and Prabal Rana easily surmised that 'the die had turned'. Still, in keeping with the prevailing decorum, both the courtiers respectfully bowed at the feet of Ranabahadur, offering their allegiance. But, as if they were being rewarded for their civilized behaviour, both Damodar and Prabal were arrested forthwith—on the orders of Ranabahadur and as per the plan of Bhimsen Thapa and others. Both were handcuffed and their feet shackled. Following the arrest of these two courtiers, all their associates fled the scene.

Then Ranabahadur, accompanied by the associates who had returned with him from Benaras, went over to Tundikhel near the Lumadhi temple and spent the first night in the tents that had been set up for him. Damodar and Prabal were kept in a nearby inn under close observation. Subsequently, on the advice of Bhimsen Thapa and Sherbahadur, Ranabahadur got Rajrajeswori arrested, issuing the arrest order from Tundikhel. He also freed from jail Subarnaprabha, Bom Shah, Bakhtabarsingh Basnyat, Ranajit Pande and others; and, barring Subarnaprabha, all the courtiers recovered their respective positions in the administration. Ranodyot Shah regained the title of 'senior minister', while Sherbahadur Shahi became the second senior minister, and Pran Shah and Bom Shah, ministers. Ranganath Poudel was appointed the royal preceptor. Bakhtabarsingh, Narsingh, Tribhuvan and a few others were appointed as ministers. Amarsingh Thapa (Senior) and his sons were retained in their posts. However, Jashapou Thapa was dismissed, and his allowance was allotted to Bhimsen Thapa. Bhimsen's father and brother, Amarsingh Thapa (Junior) and Nayansingh Thapa were appointed ministers in the new council.

All this was carried out under the initiative of Ranabahadur though he had no legal authority to run the state administration. At this time, Girban had his position intact as king, while Sherbahadur was active as the monarch's closest aide, and Ranajit Pande had been nominated to the high position of senior minister.

After all these actions were taken, any legal authority vested with Ranabahadur was notable by its absence. In fact, everything was happening as per the wishes and aspirations of Bhimsen Thapa—Ranabahadur was merely playing second fiddle to Bhimsen. And had Bhimsen so wanted, he could have got for himself the position of the seniormost minister, but because he deemed it unwise to assume the position right away, he contented himself with the position of an ordinary minister and appointed Ranajit Pande, the father-in-law of one of his brothers, to the elevated position. Ranajit Pande was someone who was ever willing to carry out Bhimsen's orders.

Following the arrest of Rajrajeswori and Damodar, the old

court was automatically dissolved. Thereafter, the restraints that had been put on Ranabahadur in meddling in the affairs of the state by the trust document, signed while handing over the state authority to King Girban, were rendered invalid. Meanwhile, with scant regard to post or protocol, Bhimsen began to fully exercise control over the country's administration. Unhindered and in the name of the ex-king, Bhimsen began to discharge all administrative responsibilities, while Ranabahadur continued to remain entrenched in seeking the pleasures of life.

Around the third or the fourth day of their arrest, Damodar and Prabal lay awake at the basement of the near-derelict inn beside the Lumadhi temple, reflecting on the calamity that lay in store for them. With the security guards fast asleep outside the room, Prabal proposed, 'This is the opportune time, let's run away.' 'But where do we go?' asked Damodar. 'The firangis [British] are our enemy; it is better to die here than to seek shelter with them. Yes, if we could ever make it to Palpa, we would get support from King Prithvipal Sen there, and our lives could be secure. But this way, we will bring about a break-up of this nation built by the blood and sweat and sacrifices of my father, Kalu Pande, and my brother Bamsaraj Pande, who even risked their lives to [achieve] this end; eventually, the firangis will benefit. Better to sacrifice one's life than live a life of treason.'

'No, we have to save our lives by escaping,' said Prabal. 'If you survive, you have more chances of serving the nation. If you are alive, the possibilities are galore.' But Damodar was unenthusiastic about the idea. Prabal made enough entreaties, yet Damodar remained unmoved. In the end, Prabal declared,

'If you think it is unwise to flee, may you have peace in your next life; I, for one, will run away and seek peace in this life itself.'

At daybreak, pretending to answer the call of nature, Prabal, accompanied by a soldier, went to a nearby field and escaped from there. On the charge of letting him go, one jamadar and a soldier were put to death the next day. Damodar and the others, who had already been sentenced to death, were subjected to more cruel torture thereafter.

For a couple of days after his return from Benaras, Ranabahadur had lived a quiet life. But on 7 March 1804, he abandoned the saffron robes and, attired in full royal regalia, entered the royal palace. Nobody dared to protest this unlawful act; instead, most of the nobility encouraged him. Then the first thing that Ranabahadur did was to deal with Damodar, who had been inhumanely tortured for the past twelve days. There was some fear that if Damodar was moved to some other place, the army would take notice and rise in revolt out of sympathy for him. So, as planned by Bhimsen Thapa and others, he was not shifted anywhere but was brutally beheaded at the cremation ground near Lumadhi, on 13 March 1804. Also hacked to death there were his eldest son, Ranakeshar Pande, and second son, Gajakeshar Pande. Then, ex-minister and treasurer Bhim Khawas and one of his sons were cut to death in the Bisnumati River, while another son was left to drown in the pond of Taudaha in Chobhar. Another son of Bhim's had his feet tied and he was hung upside down on a tree for three days at Chhauni; he did not die but was later beheaded. Subba Shankhadhar Khawas was buried in a pit up to his shoulders; his hair was coated with wax and set on fire. Also beheaded were Sirdar Indraman Khatri, watchman Samansingh and Subedar Maandhan. No charge or case had been brought against any one of them nor had any verdict of punishment been announced. Among those who survived this ordeal were Damodar's other two sons, Karbir Pande and Ranajung Pande (both below the age of fourteen), and his grandsons—they could save their lives only because they fled. All of Damodar's property was confiscated and all the women of his family—hapless indeed—were banished from Kathmandu.

By ordering the brutal murder of an innocent man like Damodar Pande, who had fought many battles fraught with risks, who had contributed immensely to and worked hard for the expansion of the kingdom, and was a person known for his sense of patriotism and loyalty, Ranabahadur and his cohorts had without doubt committed an exceedingly inhuman and despicable act. They were also as inhuman and despicable in the brutal way in which they had done away with several other courtiers. One feels that the least that could have been done was to remember the matchless services rendered to the nation by Damodar's illustrious father, Kalu Pande, brother Bamsaraj and others. But who was there to recall all this? The way the situation unfolded, utter disregard was shown to the conscientious dictum of Prithvinarayan Shah: 'Never ever kill your own brothers or courtiers.' How can one describe such acts, except by calling them the height of inhumanity?

After annihilating their rivals, Bhimsen and his ilk now started instigating Ranabahadur to wipe out the kings of Palpa and Garhwal. Both these states had already come under the influence of the Nepalese kingdom, with their kings acting as friends and well-wishers. While Ranabahadur had been living in Benaras, these states had continued to honour their pledge of loyalty to the royal palace in Kathmandu, without offering any service to the ex-king. That was their crime, if it could be called so. Ranabahadur invited the King of Palpa, Prithvipal Sen, to Kathmandu, by offering him a marriage proposal: 'I will marry your sister. So please come here along with my bride.' On his arrival, Prithvipal and his brother Ranabahadur Sen were arrested and, in a further act of betrayal, Nepalese forces were sent to seize their state. Not long after that, an attack was mounted on Garhwal and the state was annexed. The Garhwali king Pradyumna Shah was killed in the fighting, while one of his brothers was held prisoner. His son and another of his brothers survived by fleeing.

At this time, one of Damodar's sons held the position of Governor of Kumaon. On Ranabahadur's orders, he was arrested by Amarsingh Thapa, who was in fact sent out to mount an attack on Garhwal. Damodar's son was then sent to Kathmandu, but he died on the way, unable to bear the pain and the weight of the shackles on his feet and chains around his neck.

As for Queen Rajrajeswori, after being interned in Kathmandu for a few months, she was shunted out of the capital barefoot, on 21 May 1805, and forced to live the life of an exile in the community of the Sherpas in the Helambu hills, towards the north-east of the capital.

Amidst all this, it was the young princes who suffered

the most brutal acts of injustice—and these princes were innocent and harmless on all counts. Balabhadra Shah, who had accompanied Rajrajeswori to Benaras as her patron, had earlier died on the way back to Kathmandu. But his patronage of the queen was considered a crime. He had no offspring, so three of his nephews, including Birbhadra Shah, had inherited his property. Then there was Kulchandra Shah, the eleven-year-old son of ex-minister Dalmardan Shah (he had fathered a son in old age), living quietly off his inherited property. These princes had all along kept themselves aloof from the politics of the palace. But while living in Benaras with Swamiji, the likes of Bhimsen Thapa and Ranganath Pandit had conceived a plan to seize the property of these princes, in particular their splendid mansions. So now, on the orders of Ranabahadur, all the innocent princes, including Birbhadra, Bhimpratap Shah, Bhimrudra Shah and Kulchandra were blinded and imprisoned in the palace. The mansion of Birbhadra, Bhimpratap Shah and Bhimrudra Shah was awarded to Bhimsen Thapa, while Ranganath Pandit obtained Kulchandra's mansion as his share.

As regards the fate of Prabal, after escaping from the inn near the Lumadhi temple, he had disguised himself as a hermit and had taken shelter with the landlord Raja Birkesharsingh of Bettiya. As Prabal was Damodar's brother, the raja had no hesitation in providing refuge to a man who was apparently in trouble. Later, Damodar's wife and some of her children, who were exiled from Kathmandu, also reached there, seeking shelter. On meeting Prabal there, they narrated to him the heart-rending happenings in Kathmandu, including the slaying of Damodar.

Later, in Benaras, Prabal met Subba Deenanath Upadhyaya Sapkota, who had been a vakil in Calcutta since the time of Prithvinarayan Shah. Sapkota had chosen to spend the rest of his old age in Benaras after he had been replaced as vakil by Krishna Pandit, a brother of Ranganath Pandit's, on the orders of Bhimsen Thapa. At that time, hearing of the political events in Nepal, Sapkota definitely did not want to return to his homeland. And, as if to apprise him of the details of the happenings in the Nepalese capital, Prabal had run into him in Benaras.

When the two met, Sapkota, with his grey beard and moustache, was sixty-eight years old, while Prabal was fifty-five. Sad and forlorn, the two, sitting on cots matted with ropes, chatted with each other in an ordinary room of an ordinary building somewhere in Benaras. Prabal gave Sapkota the details of all the events in Nepal, starting from the return of Ranabahadur from Benaras to his own daring escape.

After hearing about all the injustices and wrongdoings, Deenanath said, 'As a consequence of such a family feud, the British will mutilate the Nepalese kingdom, and Nepal may even lose its independence.' To this, Prabal responded, saying, 'If Nepal faces an attack of the firangis, we will fight them, prove our valour and bravery, and safeguard the motherland, and, if needed, we will even come to an agreement with Bhimsen Thapa.' 'Bravo, this is what is called patriotism!' Deenanath exclaimed.

Unpublished, written around 1952

Three

The Slaying of Ranabahadur: Bhimsen Rules the Roost

Agrand and magnificent mansion stood at the south-west corner of Tundikhel in Kathmandu, where Balabhadra Shah, son of the late Mahoddamkirti Shah, who was the second brother of Prithvinarayan Shah, lived with his nephews. The mansion stood inside a walled compound spread over a vast area of land. Bhimsen Thapa had set his eyes on it.

After the passing away of Balabhadra, Bhimsen Thapa forcibly occupied the mansion after confiscating the property of the nephews—these innocent nephews had their eyes put out, and were then arrested on the charge of taking the side of Queen Rajrajeswori.

Another splendid mansion stood on the main road that led to the present-day New Road from Indrachowk Square. The owner of this house, Dalmardan Shah, the third brother of Prithvinarayan Shah, had died by this time, leaving behind his wife and their eleven-year-old son, Kulchandra Shah; both lived in this mansion. Many nobles and courtiers had set their eyes on this house. Sherbahadur Shahi, who had played a

crucial role in bringing Ranabahadur back from Benaras, was
one of the courtiers coveting the mansion. But, following a
heated debate on who should get it, Bhimsen Thapa denied
the mansion to Sherbahadur; instead, it was given to Pandit
Ranganath Poudel. A rift, nay open enmity, arose between
Bhimsen and Sherbahadur, which grew worse in due course
as the two ambitious youths emerged as competitors in the
domain of Nepalese politics.

No authority as such was vested in Ranabahadur by the
new Courtiers' Council installed after his return from Benaras.
He was neither the king nor a minister, nor was he the regent.
Girbanyuddhabikram Shah continued to be the king. But
Rajrajeswori, who had been acting as the regent of the minor
king, had been interned, while Damodar Pande had been done
away with. His replacement, Ranajit Pande, though the chief
kazi and prime minister, exercised no authority. So, while on
the surface it looked as if Ranabahadur was the principal
authority, it was Bhimsen Thapa who ran the affairs of the
state, almost single-handedly. Except on matters that would
tend to undermine the interest of the nation, the ministers
generally took orders from Bhimsen Thapa. Ranabahadur
firmly believed that the nobles and courtiers would do
nothing to harm his interests. But Sherbahadur Shahi, for one,
continued to be infuriated with Ranabahadur because of the
latter's special affection towards Bhimsen Thapa.

Sherbahadur had done his utmost to secure the homecoming
of his brother Ranabahadur, because he believed that the state
authority would then fall in the hands of Ranabahadur, which
would thus help him to enhance his position as well as give

him the power to influence people. But, as it turned out, it was Bhimsen Thapa, not Ranabahadur, who went on to assume all the authority—Ranabahadur merely became a toy in Bhimsen's hands. Sherbahadur was now an increasingly restless man, one who saw in front of him a bleak future. As for Bhimsen Thapa, the clever man that he was, he clearly understood what was going on in Sherbahadur's mind. He realized that in order to take full control over the state administration, he had to remove Sherbahadur and his supporters, who were posing obstacles in the way. Bhimsen now hatched a plan under which Ranabahadur would pronounce the death sentence on his adversary.

Meanwhile, the victory campaign continued in the west, and in the process, small states such as Sirmor, Kahaloor and Handoor—all lying towards the west of Garhwal—had been subdued. Except for its main fort, the state of Kangada too had come under the jurisdiction of the Nepalese kingdom. As to the question of whether Bhimsen Thapa contributed to these conquests in any way, the answer would be in the negative. Behind these achievements were the high morale and motivation of the Nepalese soldiers fighting in the battlefields. Yet, in Kathmandu, Bhimsen and his coterie of nobles and courtiers were making the most out of the successes in the expansion campaign.

In the palace itself, following the exile of Queen Rajrajeswori and the internment of Subarnaprabha, the need for a queen mother was felt, if only to act as the regent of King Girban who was a minor. Towards the fulfilment of this need, Ranabahadur summoned to Kathmandu a minor sister of Prithvipal Sen, the King of Palpa, as a bride. For unknown reasons, however, Ranabahadur did not marry her; instead, he chose a Rajput girl named Chandrabati as his bride.

All this while, Bhimsen Thapa continued to pull the strings of power. On the midnight of 26 February 1806, as per a plan charted out by Bhimsen, 'Swami Maharaj' Ranabahadur Shah assumed the position of *mukhtiyar* (prime minister), with the approval of King Girban. And seemingly, Bhimsen had won Sherbahadur's consent. Questions can still be asked about this particular plan of Bhimsen Thapa's: why was Ranabahadur denied of powers for nearly two years since his return from Benaras, prompted to assume the premiership and act as the regent? Legally speaking, Ranabahadur's formal assumption of the office of prime minister amounted to placing restraints on the authority of Bhimsen. So, why did Bhimsen accept a diminished status of power? Around this time, records also say that Ranabahadur married another Kshatriya girl named Lalita. Who was this Kshatriya girl, later known as Queen Lalittripurasundari and who became a lifelong well-wisher of Bhimsen Thapa? Why did Ranabahadur marry her at that particular time? Moreover, why did she not perform Sati when her husband died? All these questions have remained unanswered till date.

Some three weeks after the assumption of premiership, on the night of 14 March 1806, following the orders of Ranabahadur, soldiers were sent to arrest Tribhuvan Pradhan (Khawas), Sherbahadur's maternal uncle. Pradhan was charged with embezzling Rs 18,000 from the treasury and wrongly giving permit to the British to open a trade mart at Kirtipur;

his mansion and other property were then confiscated that very night. And then, without any deliberations on the charges brought against him, an order was issued for Pradhan to be beheaded by the Bisnumati River; he was then taken to the slaughter ground, accompanied by a butcher, Jayant Rana. Actually, Pradhan was innocent and, even if not, the charges against him should have come earlier, some two years ago. Bhimsen Thapa had taken this vile step in order to take revenge on Pradhan's nephew, Sherbahadur Shahi. Now Pradhan, like the proverbial drowning man clutching at a straw, wrote an appeal to Ranabahadur and gave it to the butcher, who thought it was important and should be delivered. In the appeal, he stated: 'If the matter is placed before all nobles and courtiers, it would be known who all were involved; I am not the only offender, there are others too.' This aroused Ranabahadur's curiosity; he wanted to know who else was involved, so he issued orders for Pradhan to be brought back from the slaughter ground to subject him to a re-examination. Pradhan was then held in detention at his confiscated house.

Tribhuvan Pradhan was possibly the grandson of the veteran kazi Dhanawanta Pradhan, an old-timer of Patan. But now, attempts were being made to trap him by accusing him of being a criminal and, through him, Sherbahadur and his brother, Bidur, too. After receiving Pradhan's appeal, Ranabahadur, on the advice of Bhimsen, sent a summons, saying: 'The Royal Council is meeting at the residence of Tribhuvan Pradhan this evening; all nobles and courtiers please be present.' The summons was sent to all the prominent nobles and courtiers. By this time, Ranabahadur had granted Pradhan's confiscated mansion—which presently stands at Ranamukteswor—as a baksheesh to Chitrabati, the mother of Kirtimansingh. It's not known why, on the day of the proposed council meeting, Ranabahadur had his evening meal at this mansion though his own residence was not far away from there.

Generally speaking, as convention would have it, the Nepalese royal palace held meetings and deliberations, or even court proceedings on murder or assassination, at night. A few years earlier, Bamsaraj Pande had been slain at a night-time meeting. The 26 April meeting, too, was set as a late-night event, and Sherbahadur and Narsingh Gurung had been invited as special participants. Meanwhile, the army had been given orders to use force and even arrest the duo if they showed any reluctance to attend the meeting. However, both Sherbahadur and Narsingh willingly presented themselves at the meeting, accompanied by their bodyguards.

Soon after the meeting began, chaired by Ranabahadur, Bhimsen walked out quietly, saying, 'I want to have my meal.' Then, addressing the nobles and courtiers present, Ranabahadur asked: 'On the embezzlement of money by Tribhuvan Pradhan, have you all done it together, or what is it? Who was the enemy that was defeated, by using the money? Which country did you win over? Why did you spend this money to drive me away to Kashi? Why did you allow the British to open a trade house in Kirtipur, aimed at preventing me from returning from there [Benaras]? Have you all committed the offence or not?'

Ranabahadur's questions were especially directed to Sherbahadur and Narsingh Gurung. And watching all this from a corner of the room was a hapless Tribhuvan Pradhan, bound in ropes. Pradhan was unable to furnish the detailed accounts of the 18,000 rupees that had been spent; and nor were any of the nobles and courtiers present at the meeting able to give any explanation on the matter. No business house had been opened in Kirtipur, and neither did any courtier or official issue permission for it. So, the nobles and courtiers stood there speechless, unable to give any reply to Ranabahadur's questions.

Almost all the prominent nobles and courtiers were present at the meeting. But Ranabahadur's focus was solely on Tribhuvan Pradhan, Sherbahadur Shahi and Narsingh Gurung. Sherbahadur could now clearly see that he had fallen into Bhimsen's trap. Trembling with fear and trepidation, he did however dare to raise his head and ask Ranabahadur: 'Does this charge fall on me; am I implicated?' 'Yes, it surely does,' Ranabahadur snapped back.

The meeting was taking place in a spacious veranda towards the south side of the mansion. As it was summertime, in one of the corners of the veranda lay jars of drinking water as well as mugs. Extremely tormented by the false charge levelled against him, Sherbahadur now rose to his feet and walked over to the corner, gulping two mugfuls of water.

As soon as Sherbahadur returned to the meeting, Ranabahadur, who had intently watched the former rehydrate himself, contemptuously said: 'Looks like you have turned into pulp.' Infuriated by this satirical remark, Sherbahadur walked out to the corner once again and drank one more mug of water; then he returned to the meeting and stood right in front of Ranabahadur. Exactly at this moment, a jackal howled in the garden outside, and everybody present pricked his ears to the sound. Now Sherbahadur drew his sword from its sheath hung from his waist and unexpectedly charged at Ranabahadur. (By this act, Sherbahadur had transformed himself into an assailant.) The sword, aimed at the neck of Ranabahadur, pierced his stomach instead, felling him instantly. All this was taking place in dim candlelight. Now, putting out the light, Sherbahadur made a futile attempt at escaping from the scene.

The blood-drenched Ranabahadur asked Balnarsingh Kunwar for help. Bom Shah was also present there. Together, he and Balnarsingh overpowered Sherbahadur, and Balnarsingh went on to instantaneously behead Sherbahadur, with a swipe of his sword. Also beheaded was Sherbahadur's brother-in-law who had accompanied him but had stayed behind downstairs in the courtyard. Bom Shah sustained some minor injuries in the melee. All this while, Bhimsen was still enjoying his meal in the kitchen, least bothered about whether the accused would get justice or not. Nor did he seem to be really concerned about Ranabahadur's safety and security. So the question is inevitable: why did Bhimsen, under the pretext of taking his meal, absent himself from such an important meeting chaired by Ranabahadur, for such a long time? It can be gleaned that Bhimsen's disappearance at the crucial hour was part of his secret plot of convening the council meeting, which resulted in the bloodletting.

On hearing about the violence and the killing, Bhimsen, led by an oil-lit torch, rushed to the scene. It was a horrible sight indeed. Ranabahadur lay bleeding on the ground, almost unconscious. In those days, the loud musical instrument *karnal* was played to call the army to assemble, particularly when disaster struck, and when circumstances ruled out the playing of the bugle. Accordingly, that very night, Bhimsen gave orders for the instrument to be played and got the soldiers assembled. Then followed his harsh order: 'Let nobody get out of this building under any circumstances.' Then, two bodyguards of Sherbahadur's were beheaded in the veranda itself. Three bodies, including that of Sherbahadur's, were hurled down to the courtyard below. Meanwhile, as he was being carried in a bed down to the courtyard, Ranabahadur breathed his last. His unexpected death came at the age of thirty-one, a victim of a conspiracy. His mortal remains were sent to Pashupati Aryaghat for cremation that very night.

After dispatching the body of Ranabahadur for the funeral rites, Bhimsen Thapa gave orders to detain Tribhuvan Pradhan and Narsingh Gurung at the army barrack nearby. Then, securing himself in the company of soldiers, and accompanied by Ranganath Pandit, Ranajit Pande, Bahadur Bhandari and Balnarsingh Kunwar, Bhimsen departed for the royal palace. Arriving at the palace, he lost no time in giving orders that the army be promptly sent to arrest Bidur Shahi, the brother of Sherbahadur, from the former's residence. At this time, Prithvipal Sen, the King of Palpa, and his brother Ranabahadur Sen had also been deceitfully placed under house arrest at the royal palace in Patan. Both the innocent men were brought to the capital that night. Moreover, that very night, Bhimsen sent horsemen to Queen Rajrajeswori too, to bring her back to Kathmandu. Rajrajeswori was then living in exile in Helambu. Bhimsen thought it important to remove her so that there would be no obstacle in his path towards capturing complete power.

Imprisoned by then were Bidur Shahi, Tribhuvan Pradhan, Narsingh Gurung, King Prithvipal Sen and his brother Ranabahadur Sen. Did these people together play any role in the assassination of Ranabahadur or not? Was any of them involved in it, and if so, in what way? Questions such as these were neither raised nor deliberated upon. Yet, all these men were beheaded one by one at the Bhandarkhal Garden inside the royal palace the next day. Even the minor sons of Bidur Shahi were denied their lives, while not just the sons but also the grandsons of Gurung and Pradhan were beheaded by the banks of the Bisnumati River. Their daughters and daughters-in-law too met a similar fate. The King of Palpa was cut down at the Bhandarkhal Garden, along with his eighteen bodyguards, all innocent of any wrongdoing. All these victims were denied their traditional cremation rights; their dead bodies were tied with ropes and dragged in the most demeaning way to the riverbank and left there for jackals and vultures to feast on. Thirteen courtiers, including Jagat Khawas, were hacked to death the next day, also at the same riverbank. The wives and daughters of Bidur and Sherbahadur were handed over to the Podes (low-caste latrine cleaners). All their property was confiscated.

Rajrajeswori, who was brought to Kathmandu on the ninth day, craved a glimpse of the minor King Girban. But she was denied permission. She was subsequently burnt to death as the Sati of Ranabahadur, along with fourteen of her lady attendants, by the side of the Salinadi River in

Sankhu. Ranabahadur's mistress in Benaras, who had arrived in Kathmandu on the fifteenth day of his death, met with a similar fate. Thus, in the two-week-long spell of killings, sixteen innocent women were burnt to death as Satis, while some seventy-seven men were beheaded. And those who survived had tales to tell of the torture, pain, agony and grief to which they had been subjected.

On hearing about Ranabahadur's murder, Maiya Bilaskumari, the daughter of Prithvinarayan Shah and Queen of the Salyan state, had rushed to Kathmandu. There she heard through the grapevine that Bhimsen was chiefly responsible for the murder; in fact, she even blurted this out inadvertently once. As a result, the military was summoned and she was driven out of the capital on 25 May 1806. She was promised an annual allowance of Rs 1400 and dumped at Falabang of Salyan. Her state was annexed to Nepal. What was more, the land Prithvinarayan gave her as dowry was confiscated, with no explanation given.

The massacre had its fallout in Kumaon in the far west too. At this time, Ritubarna Thapa was in Almoda, acting as its governor. Also staying there was Birbhadra Thapa, a relative of Bhimsen's. On Bhimsen's insistence, Birbhadra sent Ritubarna to Doti, where he was put to death.

By now, Bhimsen Thapa, having annihilated all his rivals, had emerged as the most powerful figure in Nepal. None was left to question his autocratic conduct. He then acquired the office of the prime minister from King Girban. He also got the king to issue an order that said: 'Henceforth, all chautaras and kazis should follow the directives of Bhimsen Thapa.' The official red seal, or lalmohar, was affixed on the order.

As for Ranabahadur's widow Lalittripurasundari, who had all along favoured Bhimsen, she had been spared the jaws of Sati. Later, she was accorded the status of Queen Mother and appointed regent of the minor king; King Girban was eight years old at the time. However, Regent Tripurasundari was least concerned about the affairs of the state, preferring to remain in Bhimsen's shadow. The only task she was entrusted with was affixing the royal seal of approval on the documents prepared and presented on the orders of the prime minister. Bhimsen was running the affairs of the state unhindered and single-handedly. There were some nobles and courtiers around, but as his nominees they could only be obedient followers.

While the murder of Ranabahadur and the crushing of all the old-time courtiers had left the field wide open to Bhimsen and his cohorts, they themselves were, by all counts, immature and inexperienced. With them in power, the traditional values of qualification, experience and contribution were thrown to the wind. Nor was anyone's contribution a factor to be reckoned with any more. As a consequence, in the year 1814, Nepal was unexpectedly drawn into a war with the British, and the country suffered mutilation.

At the site of the veranda of the Kathmandu mansion of Tribhuvan Pradhan, where Ranabahadur had breathed his last, Bhimsen Thapa built a splendid temple dedicated to Lord Shiva. The temple is still famous as the temple of Ranamukteswor.

After the general began his rule, there has been no justice. A lot of resources have gone waste; bribe-taking has grown rampant. Earlier, there was no practice of bribery. Nowadays, all courtiers take bribes. Some fifteen or sixteen years ago, three persons, namely Brajanath Mishra, Bijayasingh Shahi and Sarbajit Pande, had tried to hatch a plot to deny the general state authority as well as the power of dismissal. But the general got wind of the plot in advance and beheaded Sarbajit Pande. Brajanath Mishra was exiled to Madhesh, while Bijayasingh Shahi was shackled, jailed and later murdered.

The story above of the events leading to the murder of Ranabahadur is based on a historic document called an *arjipatra* (petition) in those days. (The passage above is from this petition.)

The petition was possibly written from Nuwakot. Presently, it is found at the India Office Library in London. In the original copy, words, sentences and even paragraphs are joined together without space. Here an attempt was made to separate them for the benefit of the readers. Though it is written in the Devanagari script of the Nepali language, many words are spelt like their counterparts in the Newari language, so, it seems, it was written by a Newar. Also, some minor corrections were made in the spelling of the words.

It is not clearly mentioned who this petition is addressed to. Yet, it can be safely presumed that it was addressed to the king, as the prevailing practice prohibited petitioning to anyone other than the king. Clearly, the writer chose a ghost name, out of fear of the then powerful ruler Bhimsen Thapa. Most likely, it was the handiwork of a certain *newardhami* (village physician), a member of the Dhami community that had started living in the Bhairabi temple in Nuwakot since the time of the Malla kings.

No mention has been made of the year the petition was written, but based on a tally of the days, weeks and months mentioned, it seems it was written on 11 July 1832. By this time, King Rajendrabikram Shah, who had taken over the reins of power following the demise of Girbanyuddhabikram, would have been nineteen years old and would naturally have shown interest in knowing and finding out about his ancestors. So, it can also be assumed that the Nuwakot physician wrote the petition on the directive of the king to 'present (the facts) in detail'.

But how did this petition land in the India Office Library of Britain? We hear that loads of manuscripts and documents written in the Nepali language and on Nepalese paper, which were in the hands of the then British Resident B.H. Hodgson, are safe in the library, in some 104 big volumes. This petition is stored in Volume No. 52. But how did Hodgson get hold of this petition in the first place? That too would be interesting to know.

Although the writer had kept his identity a secret for fear of retribution by Bhimsen Thapa, the petition first fell into Bhimsen's hands, before reaching King Rajendra. A court was moved against the writer, and it punished him. I personally think Hodgson got this petition from the then judge of the court, Sardar Vajsingh Rayamajhi.

In the petition, the Dhami has briefly narrated the incidents that took place in Nepal over the span of thirty-two years, from 1800 to 1832. As the incidents had been recalled and then jotted down many years after the actual events themselves, they are not necessarily in the correct chronological order. In some cases, the details are missing, while in others, the details that should have been mentioned first are given later. All this is perfectly understandable, as it is a work of recollection. But before discovering such a document, I had never seen or found such a detailed and lively description of the slaying of Ranabahadur and the killings that followed as well as a clear narration of the assassination of Kirtimansingh, as is presented in the petition. Nowadays, Damodar Pande is viewed as the murderer of Kirtimansingh, while the actions of Ranajit Pande are covered up. But this petition presents an opposite picture. Beyond doubt, this petition holds great significance in the annals of Nepalese history.

Unpublished, written around 1970

Four

The Fall of Bhimsen Thapa

Following the demise of Ranabahadur, Bhimsen Thapa rose to become the principal figure and unopposed autocrat of Nepal. He made Ranabahadur's third wife, Lalittripurasundari, the regent of the infant king. With the eight-year-old Girban on the throne, the regent queen favouring Bhimsen, and most of the other senior nobles and courtiers pulverized, Bhimsen had taken unto himself unbridled authority.

Legally speaking, he had assumed only the position of prime minister; this was courtesy an edict from the minor king, which said: 'Henceforth, all chautaras and kazis should follow the directives of Bhimsen Thapa.' With this edict, while the king and the regent enjoyed a higher status than Bhimsen, all the other nobles and courtiers were left to serve as subordinates.

The war between Nepal and the British East India Company is known as the single-most important political event that occurred during the administration of Bhimsen Thapa. A master conspirator he may have been, but Bhimsen lacked diplomatic acumen. He failed to grasp the largely deceitful political strategies of the British. While corruption was rife, the administration of unified Nepal, which now spread from the Tista in the east to beyond the Alaknanda in the west, cried out for reforms so as to bring about progress and prosperity to the nation. But Bhimsen utilized most of his time and resources to augment his own power and riches as well as those of his family. The need to strengthen and make more efficient the state administration was perpetually overlooked.

During this time, controversy arose over the restricted areas of land earmarked as the Pragannas in Butwal province, and Nepal was left with two options: go to war by accepting the challenge posed by the British or follow a policy of appeasement. The subject was extensively discussed at the Courtiers' Council. As Nepal was not prepared for a war, most of the council members favoured a peace agreement with the British, even if it meant giving up the lands that were under dispute. But an arrogant and inexperienced Bhimsen chose a military solution.

Bhimsen had no battlefield experience. He had never seen the passes or entry points in the remote regions of the kingdom, areas that were mostly dilapidated. It was inevitable therefore that the British would beat Nepal in the battlefields by virtue of possessing a large and highly trained army. And this is exactly what happened. A Nepal that had added new territories to it was forced into dismemberment.

A few months after the war, on 20 November 1816, King Girbanyuddhabikram Shah suddenly died at the age of nineteen, and the throne fell vacant for sixteen days until his son and heir apparent Rajendrabikram Shah ascended it on 6 December that year. At this time, Rajendra, born on 7 December 1813, was just three. The serious question to ask is: why was the throne kept vacant for so many days while the prevailing tradition prohibited such a vacuum even for a single day? During this period of time, three significant events seem to have taken place. While Girban's elder wife, Siddhilaxmidevi, performed the Sati, his second wife, Gorakshyarajyalaxmidevi, (mother of King Rajendra) also died suddenly, fourteen days after Girban. Meanwhile, a notification was received that the East India Company government would return to Nepal the Butwal district of the Terai region and six other districts to its east, including Parsa, Bara and Rautahat—these districts had earlier been ceded by Nepal under the Sugauli Treaty.

It appears that Bhimsen Thapa forced Siddhilaxmi to perform the Sati because he thought she posed a big threat to him—if Siddhilaxmi had lived on, she would have staked her claim to be the regent of the new monarch, and would have also enjoyed the other powers that had till then been vested with Queen Lalittripurasundari. Such a line of reasoning seems cogent, but what remains shrouded in mystery even now is why Rajendra had to wait till his mother's death to ascend the throne. As the governor general's notice on the returning of seven districts to Nepal was received on the day Rajendra ascended the throne, it can be assumed that his enthronement took place due to pressure from the British. And Rajendra was crowned only after ensuring that the 'Queen Grandmother' Lalit, who had favoured Bhimsen all along, remained the undisputed regent to the monarch. This once again ensured for Bhimsen the status of being the unchallenged administrator of Nepal for a long time to come.

During his long administrative stint, Bhimsen seems to have made contributions in two areas. The first was in the field of organizing and training the Nepalese Army. During the first part of his rule, special facilities or arrangements for the training of the soldiers were non-existent. That the soldiers were able to successfully achieve the task of expanding and unifying Nepal was because of their deep sense of patriotism and unrivalled courage. But then came the humiliating defeat at the hands of the British. The major causes of the defeat had been identified as ill-maintained passes and routes, as well as the inability of the Nepalese soldiers to successfully confront their trained counterparts in the battlefields. So, Bhimsen apparently focused on the organization and training of the Nepalese Army during the second half of his administration. Earlier, no need had been felt to conduct military parades, nor had there been barracks to house the soldiers. It was Bhimsen who first conceived of the *kampu* (trained) regiment—on the lines of the British Army—for Nepal, equipping it with necessary arms, other war materials and uniforms. Later, he also seems to have paid attention to the maintenance and improvement of the passes and routes of the country.

Secondly, Bhimsen showed special interest in developing greenery and building gardens. He built gardens not only at his mansion, but in other parts of the kingdom as well. His mansion was called the Baag Mahal as it stood amid the grandeur of gardens. He also showed interest in digging ponds and lakes. Further, he paid special attention to making Kathmandu look attractive, even if it was only restricted to beautifying and enhancing the splendour of his own mansion. Of the two grand towers erected by him in front of his mansion, one was destroyed by the earthquake of 1833 during his lifetime, while the other still stands, though partly destroyed by the big earthquake of 1934. The Sundhara (Golden Conduit) built by him in front of his mansion even now stands as a testimony to his days of glory.

All this took place in the mid-1830s when Bhimsen Thapa's star shone bright. Though known as the mukhtiyar, he acted as a military general or a commander. While the bards eulogized him as a minister, the British addressed him as the prime minister in their correspondence. As the most prominent administrator of the kingdom, he commandeered a 6000-strong army.

The council of ministers appointed in Ranabahadur's time twenty-eight years ago had, by that time, considerably thinned down. The few ministers remaining in the Cabinet were rendered powerless and assigned to act as mere advisers to Bhimsen Thapa. Among them were Ranganath Pandit and Dalbhanjan Pande who were retained in the council, while Fattejung Pande was inducted into it following the death of his father, Pran Shah. Every year, the process of *pajani* (reappointment and dismissal of state officials, including officers of the military) would take place on a regular basis, and Bhimsen Thapa and all these ministers would be routinely reappointed to their respective positions. Many senior ministers, other ministers and high officials would get their appointments renewed, while others would be dismissed, transferred or replaced by new appointments.

In the case of the army, Bhimsen Thapa appointed only his brothers, nephews, other relatives and confidants to its key ranks. Accordingly, his younger brother Ranabirsingh Thapa was appointed 'commanding-colonel' and his nephew Mathbarsingh Thapa, 'colonel'. The duo would be reappointed during the pajani every year, just as many others all through the army ranks—from captains to ordinary soldiers. Soldiers who had become old and those who were incapacitated, as well as those in poor health, were routinely dismissed.

Right from the early days of Bhimsen's administration, four regiments of soldiers had been stationed at Palpa, an important gateway in west Nepal. There, too, Bhimsen gave the charge of the battalions only to his brothers and relatives, appointing them as the region's governors. Similarly, two regiments had been stationed at Silgadhi, the headquarters of Doti-Achham, where courtiers Pushkar Shah, Dakshya Shah and Jyan Shah—all Bhimsen's men—would take turns as governors. The other districts of the kingdom had, on an average, forty to fifty soldiers. In these districts, termed 'ordinary districts', officials from the families of senior courtiers such as Pande and Basnyat would be appointed governor by turn. As it was a form of military rule, the general populace remained suppressed, with nobody daring to offer any kind of opposition. A forced calm prevailed in the kingdom which had managed to ensure good relations with the British as well as the Chinese governments. It was exactly at this point of time that the meteor of Bhimsen, which had risen to its zenith, began to descend.

Until now, although Queen Grandmother Lalit was the lawful regent of grandson Rajendrabikram Shah, the powers she held were limited to the responsibility of unhesitatingly affixing the red seal to the documents that Bhimsen forwarded to her. Though she controlled the seal, she would not dare to speak out against *Jarnel Dai* [she fondly called Bhimsen, 'Brother General']. And if all this were not enough, Bhimsen posted his brother Ranabirsingh Thapa to the royal palace, just to ensure that nobody filled the ears of the queen grandmother and the king with stories against him. Should any of the courtiers want to call on the royals on some official business, it was done through Ranabirsingh who would be compulsorily present at these meetings.

King Rajendra had two wives—Samrajyalaxmi and Rajyalaxmi. Both these queens were only one year or one and a half years younger than him. The senior queen, Samrajyalaxmi, had given birth to two sons, while the junior queen had a daughter. As King Rajendra, who had just attained his adulthood, had not received a proper education because no such facilities existed then, and as he was addicted to the pleasures of life, he remained unaware of the close surveillance under which the prime minister had kept him. Both his queens, who were comparatively more conscious of their rights and duties, began to slowly but surely feel the pressures of internment—they even started complaining to the king about their predicament. Bhimsen's mansion, which was by far bigger and more splendid than the royal palace itself, also became the main hub of the courtiers and other members of the nobility. In contrast, the royal palace looked 'pale' and deserted, much to the chagrin of the young queens who heaped all the blame for their plight on Bhimsen Thapa.

Cunningly, Bhimsen had blocked almost all channels of communication to the royal palace so as to ensure that no information from outside could get in. A small channel, however, was open—a case of oversight. The palace maids used to be granted leave for eight to ten days every month during their period of menstruation—the belief was that if they stayed within the palace precincts during that time, the purity of the palace itself would be lost. Bhimsen had allowed this practice to continue, assuming that the illiterate and ignorant maids would pose no threat to him. But by this time, the palace had started showing concern in the affairs of the state, and the maids, returning from their leave, would bring to the palace an account of all that they had heard in their villages about the misdeeds and wrongdoings of the prime minister. The maids told the young queens how innocent courtiers like Minister Damodar Pande and their adult and minor sons had been killed; how innocents like Birbhadra Shah had been subjected to brutal torture, with their eyes gouged out and their property confiscated; and how Tribhuvan Pradhan and other innocent courtiers had been beheaded for no rhyme or reason. On hearing of all the brutal and inhuman acts carried out on the orders of Bhimsen, the queens had advised King Rajendra to remain on high alert against the designs of the prime minister.

In February 1832, a cholera epidemic broke out in

Kathmandu, and Queen Grandmother Lalit became one of its victims. She died a premature death on 26 February 1832. As she had been the perennial source of Bhimsen Thapa's power, her death sounded the preliminary notes of his doom. As was the norm, following the regent's death, King Rajendra's official seal fell into the hands of the elder queen, Samrajyalaxmi. The queen had been waiting for such an opportunity. Utilizing the special powers vested with the red seal, she made massive efforts to rid the palace of the unauthorized surveillance that Bhimsen had mounted. Bhimsen's brother Ranabirsingh Thapa, posted at the palace to oversee its affairs, now began to perceive the feeling of uneasiness that existed among the royals. Riveting his sight clearly on the post of prime minister, he started provoking Samrajyalaxmi against Bhimsen. When Bhimsen got wind of what his brother had been doing, he called Ranabirsingh and administered him a rebuke. But this only infuriated Ranabirsingh, who then left his job and went to live in his village, Sipamandal, some twenty miles east of Kathmandu. As Ranabirsingh's departure from the royal palace slackened the surveillance over it, Bhimsen moved to a bungalow near the palace in a bid to keep a close watch on the royal affairs himself.

During this time, King Rajendra took ill, afflicted by a minor ailment. The royal physician, Sirdar Ekdev Upadhyaya, was treating the king and, in the process, gave him some medicines. But the queens proscribed the medicines—not without a reason though. Earlier, when King Girban's wife had died fourteen days after the demise of her husband, rumours had made the rounds that she had actually been murdered—that physician Ekdev had administered her medicine mixed with poison, at Bhimsen's insistence. During that time, no one had dared to speak out against it as Bhimsen had been ruling with an iron hand. But now, with that rumour rife in palace circles, the queens clamped a ban on Ekdev's medicines. All this came as a rude shock to Bhimsen.

Later, Bhimsen's influence, power and authority were dealt a big blow when King Rajendra, on the pretext of mourning the death of Lalittripurasundari, cancelled that year's annual pajani. However, a few months later, by winning the younger queen, Rajyalaxmi, over to his side, Bhimsen succeeded in persuading the king to hold the annual reappointment-and-dismissal programme. And when the pajani was held, everything went off as planned, except that his own tenure of mukhtiyar was not renewed. Bhimsen Thapa was in a state of shock. Queen Samrajyalaxmi wanted to remove him from the post, replacing him with Pushkar Shah, a relative from her mother's side. But they did not dare to pass the order of removal itself since Bhimsen still commanded the support of most of the army officer corps. So, a few days later, he was reappointed the prime minister.

Meanwhile, following the death of Bhaktabarsingh Thapa, Bhimsen's third brother who had been the governor of Palpa district, his son Tribikram Thapa was temporarily appointed the governor. Tribikram was not happy with Bhimsen as he felt that his father had died in some kind of exile; moreover, he was unhappy that he had been denied a long-term appointment. For his part, Bhimsen was aware of Tribikram's discontent, so he was forced to call his younger brother Ranabirsingh—

whom he had earlier annoyed with a rebuke—from his village and appoint him 'junior general', before dispatching him to Palpa as the governor. Bhimsen did not fully trust Ranabir, but yet he took him in because there was nobody else who could be trusted more. During the pajani, however, King Rajendra had offered the position of the principal chautara to Pushkar Shah, thereby denying it to Fattejung Shah, much against the wishes of Bhimsen, who was not only shell-shocked but also hurt.

In the meantime, British envoys had set up permanent residence in Kathmandu after the end of the Anglo-Nepalese War of 1814–16. But, thanks to Bhimsen's extraordinary vigilance, they had had no opportunity to interfere directly in the internal affairs of Nepal. Their activities were mostly confined to hunting in the forests around the valley and watching the scenery of the magnificent Himalayas. Around this time, in January 1833 to be precise, B.H. Hodgson, who had been acting as assistant Resident for the past eight years, was appointed the British Resident of Nepal. As someone who had lived long in Kathmandu, devoting his spare time to studying Nepalese history, geography, language, culture as well as her fauna and flora, Hodgson had kept himself abreast of developments in the kingdom's socio-political sectors. Indeed, Bhimsen had shared his anguish with the British Resident when his reappointment as mukhtiyar had been stalled. On the other side, as advised by her counsellors and prompted by her own desire to get rid of Bhimsen's surveillance, Queen Samrajyalaxmi, too, had remained in touch with the envoy, keeping him regularly informed on matters that concerned her. The envoy was not averse to the idea of making the most out of the running internal feud.

However, belated though it was, it dawned on Bhimsen Thapa that mutual animosity generally bred harm. So, he initiated a practice of consulting with and seeking the approval of both King Rajendra and Queen Samrajyalaxmi on matters of running the administration of the state. Once, when portfolios were allocated in the council of ministers, the king himself took up the charge of defence, finance and foreign affairs, giving Samrajyalaxmi the charge of the department of law, the accounts office (at Kumarichowk), and other civil service departments. By this time, the queen actually had power even over the king and would discharge responsibilities that would otherwise have been entrusted to her husband. Notwithstanding all this, she was unable to disregard Bhimsen's counsel as he still commanded the support of the army. The general atmosphere—though not devoid of distrust and suspicion—was one in which mutual advice and consultations prevailed, with the result that the state administration ran smoothly.

In September 1833, a big earthquake struck Nepal, causing immense loss. The king, the queen and the prime minister worked together to offset the loss. Nearly five months later, a letter was received from Lahore seeking assistance for 'Panjabkeshari' Ranjit Singh, the King of Punjab. King Rajendra and Bhimsen Thapa responded by sending an envoy along with a *khalitapatra* (letter from one head of state to another). Envoys were also sent to Burma and Iran. King Rajendra and Bhimsen also discussed the possibility of sending an envoy to

King William IV in London, and accordingly, they decided to send Mathbarsingh Thapa there. Towards that end, a new army regiment called Singhanaad was set up under the command of Mathbar, who was promoted to the rank of junior general. Ranabirsingh Thapa, stationed at Palpa, was also promoted and given the famous title of 'full general'. Also, Mathbar's nephew Sherjung Thapa was promoted to 'commander-colonel'. During this particular year, mutual goodwill and understanding prevailed between the king and his prime minister, and Bhimsen was successful in regaining his lost authority to a certain extent.

All this while, the British Resident Hodgson was looking for an opportunity to capitalize on any animosity that might erupt between the durbar and Bhimsen. He brought up the issue of signing a treaty of commerce between Nepal and Britain. Bhimsen did not decline it outright, but during the negotiations, the terms and conditions could not be agreed upon (in the process, several drafts were written and torn up). An infuriated Hodgson thereafter concentrated his efforts on replacing Bhimsen with Fattejung Shah as the prime minister.

Meanwhile, on the Nepalese side, dates were set for the departure of Mathbarsingh to London. King Rajendra, overjoyed at the turn of events, expressed his gratitude to Bhimsen Thapa by bestowing on him the title of 'commander-in-chief' of the Nepalese Army. Mathbar left the country amid great fanfare, accompanied by a retinue of some top army brass who would proceed to London with him, and some 650 soldiers who would return from Calcutta. In Calcutta, Mathbar was expected to display a conduct of high order. Instead, he was found indulging in ostentatious behaviour, blowing away resources in an extravagant manner. A contemporary piece of writing has narrated Mathbar's activities in Calcutta thus:

> Issuing orders that his officers wear pearl-studded dresses, he [Mathbar] presented himself to the 'lath' [governor general] in grandeur. Swaggering on elephant back, he passed through the lanes of the Calcutta city throwing coins, enjoying the dance, music and spectacle of famous women and dancers, and gave away rewards and baksheesh in the name of his kingdom; he returned to Nepal and narrated all this in an audience with the king.

At that time, Sir Charles Metcalf was the acting British governor general in India. Initially, he accorded a warm welcome to Mathbar, but started cold-shouldering him after secret communications arrived from Kathmandu. Thereafter, Mathbar was denied passage to London, and Metcalf himself received at his Calcutta office the gifts and credentials meant for King William IV, with the assurance that those would be forwarded to the royal palace in London in due course. This was a severe diplomatic blow to Bhimsen Thapa. Moreover, until then, the king as well as the people of Nepal had held the belief that the British were among Bhimsen's best friends and that, because of his friendship with them, the British had shied away from taking over Nepal. But now, when Bhimsen's ambitious nephew returned from Calcutta, unable to make his way to London, the nature of the friendship between Bhimsen and the British stood exposed. A stunning blow had been delivered to the prime minister's authority. Sending Mathbar to Calcutta hurriedly without making proper arrangements for his passage as well as his passport turned out to be a mistake for which Bhimsen would pay dearly later.

During this time, Ranajung Pande, the son of Damodar Pande (who had been slain on the orders of Bhimsen), was an army captain; he had been appointed by Bhimsen on the persuasion of Ranabirsingh Thapa (Bhimsen's brother). However, despite Ranajung's rank, Mathbarsingh, known for his arrogant behaviour, would not acknowledge the captain's salute even when given with due respect. Obviously, Ranjung felt hurt at this attitude. Moreover, it was hard for him to forget the brutal killings of his father and brothers, as well as the confiscation of their property, and the fact that he had survived only because he had managed to escape. So Ranajung was waiting for an occasion, if ever it came, to wipe out Mathbar, and also his uncle Bhimsen, from the Nepalese political scene. He had also kept himself abreast of the animosity growing between Queen Samrajyalaxmi and Bhimsen. Quietly, Ranajung had forwarded assurances to the queen that he was prepared to do his utmost should his service be required to ensure the downfall of Bhimsen Thapa.

About a month after Mathbar's return from Calcutta, his widowed sister-in-law unexpectedly gave birth to a child. The child was a product of Mathbar's illicit relationship with his sister-in-law. Ranajung Pande took this incident as a golden chance and, when he revealed this secret affair in public, Mathbar was widely condemned and reviled. Then, under the pretext of going on a pilgrimage, Mathbar went to live in his ancestral home at Borlang in Gorkha, where, in a bid to cover up the scandal, Bhimsen Thapa appointed Mathbar as its governor.

Around this time, the treasury of the Nepalese kingdom ran into a severe cash crunch. While the country had been facing a difficult time, Mathbar had blown away money in dance, music and feasting in Calcutta, incurring a loss of about Rs 150,000 to the national exchequer. At that time, Queen Samrajyalaxmi had been furious with Bhimsen over what was considered a waste of resources. And, in order to placate the queen, Bhimsen had reimbursed the entire expenses of his nephew from his own personal assets. And that was why Bhimsen could renew his premiership tenure that year. However, the command of the country's military arsenal was withdrawn from Mathbar and allocated to other courtiers. This led to a dent in the military's support for Bhimsen.

Subsequently, attention was drawn to the expenditure involved in the upkeep and training of the armed forces. Bhimsen Thapa had granted land to all the civil servants as well as the military, and the crops accruing from it replaced the monthly cash emoluments. However, the army men enjoyed more income than the civil servants of equal rank; an army officer could get twice or even three times more than his basic salary depending on the price situation in the market. For example, an army captain who was allocated Rs 4000 per annum could collect more than eight to 10,000 rupees annually, based on the prevailing price situation. The palace abhorred such excessive expenses in the name of military preparations. So, both the king and the queen entrusted the royal preceptor Ranganath Pandit with the task of firming up the royal treasury by cutting down the allocations to the military and also the civil servants.

By the end of 1836, it was clear that Bhimsen's days as prime minister were numbered. His brother Ranabirsingh Thapa was one of the strong aspirants to the position. From Palpa, Ranabirsingh wrote to King Rajendra, requesting a transfer to Kathmandu. Subsequently, he was called to the capital by Queen Samrajyalaxmi, who was scheming to assemble all anti-Bhimsen courtiers in the capital. Perhaps, Captain Ranajung Pande was also assisting both the queen and Ranabirsingh in this scheme. But Bhimsen, being unaware of the plan, seemed glad about the return of his brother from Palpa. He even handed over the bulk of his responsibilities to his brother and left for his ancestral home in Borlang, saying that he would devote himself to performing religious rites.

This resolve was merely an excuse. Actually, he had gone to Gorkha in order to bring Mathbar back to Kathmandu. And when Mathbar returned to Kathmandu, the queen voiced no opposition—instead, she said she was happy about it. By this time, the king and the queen had taken control of most of the army regiments of the Kathmandu valley. However, they also knew that the regiments, created by Bhimsen and kept under his command over a long period of time, were not to be trusted fully. So when Bhimsen was away in Gorkha, a new regiment called Hanuman-Dal was formed, under the direct command of the royals.

In the meantime, Ranajung Pande was promoted to the position of minister, one who would serve as the principal aide to the king. Ranajung's house and land that had once been confiscated were now released. His brother, Ranadal Pande, was also promoted to the position of minister and sent to Palpa as the governor. However, Bhimsen Thapa, his brothers and nephews retained their respective positions. For the past six years, Bhimsen had been living in a bungalow near the royal palace, supposedly to look after its affairs. However, after Ranajung Pande—in his capacity as the principal aide—took charge of the royal palace affairs, Bhimsen was denied access to the palace. Bhimsen had lost for good the opportunity of presenting himself before the king and the queen in order to share his concerns with them.

Meanwhile, some grand excuse was being searched so that Bhimsen could be trapped in an offence that could lead to his political downfall. It was at this time that the six-month-old prince Devendrabikram Shah, son of Samrajyalaxmi, died rather unexpectedly on 24 July 1837. When the prince had first fallen sick, the physician Bhajuman Vaidya had administered him an Ayurvedic medicine called *agusti-bati*. At the time, this medicine, which contained bhang (marijuana) in a small portion, was commonly used as a digestive or to induce sleep in children. However, the physician who had treated the prince now found himself under detention on the charge of mixing *dhaturo* (the bitter seed of a wild narcotic plant widely found in Nepal and said to be poisonous) in the medicine consumed by the prince. The next day, he was charged with mixing another poison in the medicine. 'My son was poisoned to death by Bhajuman Vaidya who acted on the orders of Sirdar Ekdev Upadhyaya, who in turn had acted on the orders of Bhimsen Thapa'—so accused Queen Samrajyalaxmi.

King Rajendra concurred with the queen's charge. Thus, on this charge, Bhimsen Thapa was arrested from his bungalow near the royal palace. The arrest was carried out by the soldiers of the Hanuman-Dal regiment, and Bhimsen was immediately put in chains. Then his brothers and nephews were arrested: Gen. Ranabirsingh Thapa, Gen. Mathbarsingh Thapa, Col. Sherjung Thapa and Dalbahadur Thapa. Also held were Sirdar Ekdev Upadhyaya and his brother Eksurya Upadhyaya. All of these men were shackled and kept under strict observation; they were also subjected to brutal torture. All their property was confiscated.

Then what followed was a farce enacted at the royal palace in order to debate and ascertain the validity of the charge of murder. On the occasion, one of the accused, Bhajuman Vaidya, unable to bear any longer the inhuman torture that he had been subjected to, said: 'I administered the medicine given by Sirdar Ekdev, and not the one I had prepared.' On his part, Ekdev, even after being slapped on the face with hot iron, was not willing to confess that he had helped poison the baby prince. As for Mathbar, he was whipped one hundred times, but he stood motionless, not even once uttering a cry of pain. Subsequently, the physicians Ekdev and Eksurya, because they were Avadh Brahmins, had their heads tonsured on four sides and were thrown into prison amid tight security. Bhajuman Vaidya's skin was peeled off, his eyes gouged out, and then he was speared to death.

After the arrest of Bhimsen Thapa, King Rajendra wanted to appoint Dalbhanjan Pande as the prime minister. But on the special insistence of Queen Samrajyalaxmi, the position went to Kazi Ranajung Pande (son of Damodar Pande); he was also accorded the title of Diwan. The family of Ranajung was famous by the name Kala-Pande. But the family formed only a small group, so Ranajung was forced to give up the premiership after he failed to garner the support of all the courtiers belonging to the king's side. Then the king appointed Ranganath Pandit the prime minister, and gave him charge over one battalion of soldiers. Dalbhanjan Pande took charge of another battalion, while Ranajung was given charge over all the remaining battalions.

The previous year, Pandit Ranganath Poudel had availed himself of the authority to cut the allocations to all the officers and soldiers of the Kampu brigade. After he had introduced cash payment for half of the annual emoluments given to the army officers, huge areas of land granted as emolument had been freed, resulting in a significant rise in the income of the royal treasury. Ranganath had planned the same for the soldiers too, but the stiff opposition from Ranajung had discouraged him. Yet, because of Ranganath's plan, the large plots that had been granted to the Thapa family could be recovered from them—much to the delight of both the king and the queen. Now, on the special request and recommendation of Ranganath, the king and the queen agreed to clear both the Thapas of the charges against them in the poison case. Consequently, Ekdev and Eksurya Upadhyaya were also set free from prison. Meanwhile, barely a few days after his release from jail, Mathbarsingh Thapa became a hermit. Bhimsen went to his home at Borlang in Gorkha. Not long after, a rumour spread that a white tiger had been spotted in the jungle of the Terai. Saying that he would want to catch the tiger, Mathbarsingh left Kathmandu for the Terai and from there he fled to India.

At the pajani held that year, Queen Samrajyalaxmi appointed Kulchandra Shah, Pushkar Shah and Dalbahadur Pande as ministers. As Guru Krishnaraj Mishra too had joined her side and as Ranajung was fast befriending the army officers, the queen felt that her side was getting stronger by the day. She then appointed Ranajung Pande as prime minister.

Ranajung Pande still cherished the notion that Nepal's hilly territories 'foolishly lost' earlier by Bhimsen Thapa could be retrieved from the British by war. So, soon after becoming the mukhtiyar, Ranajung dispatched envoys carrying credentials from King Rajendra to Burma, China, Lahore and Gwalior. Maintenance and repair works were carried out on the passes and routes of the Mahabharat mountain range, while the Nepalese Army was enlarged with some 7000 fresh recruits, equipped with arms and ammunition. Thus, Ranajung emerged on the scene as an opponent of the British, at least in the eyes of Resident Hodgson. The credentials that the king had sent to those countries spoke only of the friendship between Nepal and those countries, and involved diplomatic niceties. The envoys had been briefed by the palace about the British being dangerous and that they were going to take over the whole region, and had been asked to tell the respective countries that vigilance against the British should get the topmost priority. Accordingly, the envoys discharged their responsibilities. But the King of Gwalior, Janakozi-Rao Shind, who had never lost an opportunity to court the favour of the British, leaked a distorted version of this message to the British envoy of his country. Following this, India's governor general Auckland moved his troops headed by Col. Oglender to Nepal's border, apparently holding out a threat of invasion. The British move left King Rajendra and Queen Samrajyalaxmi flabbergasted.

The Nepalese royal palace was now confronted with a serious problem: how to mend fences with the British? Protracted debates and discussions yielded no bright ideas. The palace then concluded that the return of Bhimsen Thapa from his village might help in finding a solution. Thereby, Bhimsen was called, and he duly returned to the capital.

Naturally, the Kala-Pandes such as Ranajung Pande were disheartened by the return of Bhimsen. The British governor general, however, expressed satisfaction at the changes effected at the high level of the Nepalese administration. The British troops mobilized along the Nepal border were withdrawn.

Bhimsen Thapa had been waiting all along for an appropriate time such as this. Putting forth the logic that the trust of the British should be restored anyhow, he proposed that two battalions of troops be taken away from the command of Ranajung Pande, and then one each be placed under the respective charge of Fattejung Shah and Prasadsingh Basnet. King Rajendra approved of the proposal. Earlier, two battalions of troops had already been taken off Ranajung's division. Now with two more battalions off his division, Ranajung's strength was considerably reduced. Obviously, Bhimsen had taken this step to weaken the political strength of his rival.

Queen Samrajyalaxmi was closely watching Bhimsen's

calculated moves. So she 'rolled up her sleeves' once again to counter the erstwhile mukhtiyar. The courtiers who supported Ranajung were on her side. The poison case of old was revived. What was more, two additional cases of poisoning were pulled out. A document, largely out of a fantasy book, was presented as proof. King Rajendra, simply unable to make out whether the document was genuine or fake, opted for the former. So, based on this document, physicians Ekdev Vaidya and Eksurya Vaidya were proven guilty though they had once been cleared in the baby prince's poisoning case. Again the duo was arrested; their heads were tonsured; and then they were thrown into prison. Bhimsen Thapa was also interned in a room in the basement of his bungalow and kept under strict vigilance.

Bhimsen had no son, only daughters. As for his other kin, his brother Ranabirsingh Thapa had become a hermit, while his nephew Mathbarsingh had gone over to Shimla, which was under the control of the British. So this time, both succeeded in escaping arrest. But the Thapa brothers who were living in Kathmandu, including Sherjung Thapa, were thrown into jail, along with their family members. All their property was confiscated. They were also denied the holy thread, the janai, which meant that their caste had been downgraded. The royal palace also went on to make an official announcement, stating that for the next seven generations to come, the Thapa family would not be eligible for jobs in the service of the administration.

Meanwhile, Bhimsen's second wife, who had been interned in her residence, reportedly made some remarks condemning Queen Samrajyalaxmi. When the palace heard of this, orders were issued to move her to prison so that she could be kept under strict observation. Rumours then started making the rounds in Kathmandu that she would soon be paraded in the street. On hearing this, Bhimsen was overwhelmed with grief and anxiety, even as he anticipated more insults to come. Finding that all avenues were now closed for him to be saved, he slashed his throat with the kukri that he carried on his waist, in the room where he was interned, on the evening of 22 July 1839. Thus, Bhimsen Thapa himself became a victim of the inhuman violence which he had employed as a means to deal with others right from the beginning.

The report that Bhimsen had attempted suicide reached the palace promptly, and both the king and the queen were infuriated. In his bid to kill himself, Bhimsen had only partly slit his throat, and rendered proper medication, his life could have been saved. But alas! That was not to be the case. By this time, there was no one among the courtiers who was powerful and sympathetic enough to come to his rescue. Nor were the army divisions, once created and commandeered by him, in a position to deliver help. That very day, as directed by the king and the queen, Bhimsen's half-conscious and blood-soaked body was dumped on the bank of the Bisnumati River where, some thirty-three years ago, bodies of some forty-five people, including those of Bidur Shahi and Sherbahadur Shahi as well as of King Prithvipal Sen, had been inhumanely left to be devoured by jackals, dogs and vultures. Lashed by the mid-monsoon winds and rains, Bhimsen hovered between life and death for nine days, before finally breathing his last on the river bank, on 30 July 1839, at the age of sixty-four.

As he had attempted to commit suicide, which was a punishable crime, there were to be no cremation rites for him. Bhimsen's mortal remains were fed to jackals, dogs and vultures. What was more, strict vigilance was mounted to ensure that no one lifted his body from the site. Then his wives were driven to the hills and imprisoned.

Why did Bhimsen attempt suicide? Was it the right thing for him to do? This has been a subject of debate and discussion for a long time. A document found by Mathbarsingh Thapa four years after Bhimsen's death, stated: 'The Kala-Pandes forced Gen. Commander-in-Chief Bhimsen Thapa to depart from this life by threatening him with shame and insults.' It indeed seems that his attempt to kill himself came mainly out of the fear of more insult and humiliation.

When he was in power, Bhimsen had ordered the brutal killings of many prominent persons and their family members; their property had been confiscated; and their hapless daughters and daughters-in-law handed over to the Podes. Furthermore, the bodies of all the slain courtiers had been fed to jackals, dogs and vultures. Seemingly, Bhimsen had been digging his own grave by giving orders for such heinous crimes to be committed.

The attempt to commit suicide stemmed from Bhimsen's weakness of mind, nothing else. Owing to his advanced age, he had lost much of his self-confidence; indeed, this confidence had already been shattered because of the struggles against the many obstacles of life. Bhimsen's main weakness lay in the fact that he failed to show patience and forbearance during distressful times.

Exactly at the spot on the bank of Bisnumati River where Bhimsen Thapa had breathed his last, Mathbar erected a temple of Lord Shiva, known later as Bhim-Mukteswor. The temple still stands there, reminding the Nepalese people of Bhimsen's heart-rending self-affliction and the ruthless torture that ensued.

Unpublished, written around 1959

Five

Mathbarsingh Betrayed: The Rise of Jungbahadur

During the time of Bhimsen's attempted suicide and subsequent death, Ranajung Pande was the Prime Minister of Nepal. He, however, was not a strong and efficient administrator. So, owing to the lack of a strong and effective administration, unrest, disorder, robbery and corruption raised their ugly heads in the kingdom. In such a situation, as he found himself ineffective in addressing these national woes, Ranajung Pande, who was a simple-minded man, turned almost senile, and finally went on to quit the prime ministerial post. Following his exit, on the insistence of Queen Samrajyalaxmi, Chautariya Pushkar Shah was appointed prime minister.

Pushkar Shah, though not an outright opponent of the British, did however remain vigilant. Naturally, the British disliked this approach. So Resident Hodson in his updates to his government portrayed Pushkar as one of the anti-British courtiers.

At this time, a minor incident took place in the kingdom. This was related to the eighteen land holdings in Parsa district over which the British and the Nepalese had been having some differences for quite some time. The British had started laying claim to these lands. On one occasion, around the middle of May, when a local market was being held at Sahodara—one of the places under dispute—Subba Bhakhtabarsingh Khadka sent his people to collect a levy on the market. It was purely a local affair, and the Nepalese central administration was unaware of it. However, for the British administration, this was proof of the correctness of Resident Hodgson's assessment of the situation in Nepal. As a threat to Nepal, Governor General Auckland ordered the movement of some troops, headed by Col. Oliver, to the Nepalese border. Pushkar Shah was dismayed. He had not planned to oppose the British in any way, nor had he been aware of the levy collection. Nepal then agreed to deposit the amount that had been collected as tax with Resident Hodgson, and proposed that an inquiry be held into the incident. This proposal, though it did calm the British down to a certain extent, however, received no formal reaction from them.

During this time, an unfortunate incident took place in Kathmandu. For a long time, the Nepalese administration had been giving its army corps as well as its civil servants their annual emolument in kind, not in cash. The practice used to be that, equipped with the *tirja* paper (document authorizing the collection of crops), the army corps as well as the civil servants could go about raising their allocations themselves, generally in the form of paddy, rice, millet and maize. However, owing to the prevailing political instability, no such paper had been distributed for the last two years. Moreover, during this time,

King Rajendra had authorized Ranganath Pandit and Kulraj Pande to conduct a review of the entire payment system for the military and the civil service. And these two courtiers had come to the conclusion that the land-based system of grants ought to be replaced by a cash-allocation system. The king was in agreement with this proposal. But the military, particularly the officer corps, was opposed to the plan. So one day, the military corps that had assembled at the parade ground of Tundikhel abandoned all their ammunition at the parade ground and went on to raid the houses of seven prominent courtiers— Pushkar Shah, Ranganath Pandit, Prasadsingh Basnet, Kulraj Pande and Karbir Pande—all of whom were in favour of the cancellation of the crop-based system of emolument. The army men then set on fire all the official papers and documents, including those that kept records of land holdings. In this mayhem of 21 June 1840, a then famous library housed at the residence of Ranganath Pandit in Indrachowk was also burnt to ashes.

This unexpected mutiny by the army startled King Rajendra and Queen Samrajyalaxmi. That same evening, Resident Hodgson was summoned to the palace and kept engaged in talks all night, before being released at dawn. The British envoy had been called fearing the possibility of a similar raid at the palace by the rebel soldiers. The mutiny ended after both the king and the queen, presenting themselves at the parade ground the next day, assured the army that they would dismiss the review plan.

The British held the council of ministers of the time in utter dislike, so the British envoy wanted to try and benefit from the opportunity provided by the mutiny. As for King Rajendra, when he had spoken to the military at the parade ground, he had mentioned that the nation's income had declined. But in Hodgson's communication to his government, he falsely alleged that the king had made an anti-British statement at the parade ground. So Governor General Auckland fired off a strongly worded letter of admonishment to the Nepalese administration. The letter also contained advice seeking the replacement of the existing ministers. King Rajendra initially ignored the letter, but when a second letter came as a follow-up, he felt helpless on the matter. So, as advised by the British, he appointed Fattejung Shah as the prime minister, removing Pushkar Shah from the post, on 1 November 1840. In the process, Karbir Pande and Kulraj Pande, brothers of Ranajung Pande, were shunted out of the Cabinet.

This change was exactly what Hodgson had sought. He even believed that the Nepalese had now abandoned their policy of opposing the British. And it would be wrong to question his assessment since he had been successful in putting in place an administration of his liking. However, despite the British suggestion for a complete overhaul of his administration, the king was able to offer captaincy to Karbir Pande and reappoint Kulraj Pande as the bodyguard of Crown Prince Surendra. Pushkar Shah, however, remained discarded.

By this time, the crown prince had stepped into adolescence. However, no proper arrangement was made for his education, and he was left free and unbridled. This was seen as a blunder on the part of King Rajendra and Queen Samrajyalaxmi. For that matter, King Rajendra himself was not a very intelligent person. As for the queen, she was being guided by the selfish motive of placing Surendra on the throne so that, as the queen mother, she could have a share in the exercising of state authority. Aggressive and wild-natured, Surendra had started supporting his mother. So, fearful of his wife and son—even fed up with them—King Rajendra was forced to think in terms of his own safety and security.

The dismissal of Pushkar Shah had left Queen Samrajyalaxmi feeling insulted as well as marginalized. Now, incensed with the king, she said she wanted to go on a pilgrimage to Benaras, and so departed for the Terai. King Rajendra followed close on her heels, in a bid to cajole her to return. The queen was then stopped by the British from crossing over the border and forced to return to Kathmandu. Then she revived her old proposal, which had sought from her husband the abdication of his throne: 'You should abdicate, placing Surendra on the throne. I will assume the position of the royal representative and then myself run the administration.' However, despite her pestering, the king remained unmoved as he was not yet ready to give up his throne. Again, expressing her unhappiness, she left her home for the Terai. She thought that this time too the king would follow her and persuade her to return, and then she would do so on the condition that her demand was met. However, her expectation remained unfulfilled: the king left her alone, making no attempt at persuasion. The queen was then struck by the summertime malaria of the Terai, and she had to make her way back to Kathmandu. Around this time, anybody attempting to give medication to a member of the royal family would have been undertaking a tremendous amount of risk involving loss of his life and property—should the medication fail to produce any result, it was almost certain that the physician would meet an unenviable fate. So, no physician came forward to treat the queen, and for lack of proper medication, Queen Samrajyalaxmi died on 6 September 1841, at the age of almost twenty-seven, some time after her return to Kathmandu. Before long, King Rajendra formally announced that Surendrabikram Shah would be the heir apparent.

By this time, King Rajendra had come under the spell of his second queen, Rajyalaxmi. She had indeed been greatly worried about the senior queen's proposal that Rajendra abdicate his throne. All along, she had feared that, should the king accept the senior queen's proposal, she herself and her minor sons would surely be doomed. But, as the senior queen's death became imminent, that doomsday prospect for her sons became a thing of the past. Yet, knowing what she did about the king's dissipating self-confidence, she herself started working out a plan towards his abdication. Under this plan, her son Ranendra Shah would ascend the throne in place of Crown Prince Surendra, and she herself would take control of the administration.

In the accomplishment of this plan, Crown Prince Surendra and his brother, Upendrabikram Shah, were the main obstacles. Rajyalaxmi did toy with the idea of seeking the fulfilment of her objective with the aid of King Rajendra and his confidant Fattejung, but she also knew it was vital that she enlist the support of a powerful group of courtiers. During this time, the brothers and other relatives of Bhimsen Thapa had remained sidelined, at best. As the opponents of the Kala-Pandes—who had all along taken the side of Samrajyalaxmi—the Thapas, naturally, now tried to develop close ties with Rajyalaxmi, making her think that they could be of great use to her.

By this time, the Thapas had grown into a strong and powerful group competent enough to put up a front not only against the Kala-Pandes, who were close to Crown Prince Surendra, but also against the king's close confidants such as Fattejung. Confident that the Thapa group would help her realize her objective, Queen Rajyalaxmi talked the king into releasing from prison the Thapa brothers, including Sherjung Thapa, as well as the physicians Ekdev Vaidya and Eksurya Vaidya; they were all restored to their respective positions on 16 August 1841.

Once he was restored to his position, Sherjung Thapa—who had the backing of King Rajendra's beloved queen—began to display his power. No sooner had he been freed from prison than he ordered the erection of a grand effigy of his grandfather Bhimsen Thapa, made out of *kushgrass* (the Hindus' sacred shrub). The effigy was then carried in a grand procession and cremated on 20 August 1841. The king had consented to this symbolic cremation rite, so his close associates, including Fattejung Shah, were forced to attend it.

Meanwhile, Bhimsen Thapa's stepbrother Ranabam Thapa, who had left the Thapa group to become an army captain with help from the Kala-Pande group, was imprisoned, having been convicted in a case involving the stealing of cannon. As for Minister Karbir Pande and army officer Kulraj Pande, it was difficult to remove them from their positions since they had both been assigned to serve Crown Prince Surendra. Kulraj

Pande hated the British, so he was fond of showing, for Surendra's entertainment, fictitious battle scenes between the Nepalese and the British armies, particularly scenes wherein the Nepalese soldiers beat the British Army. On hearing of such enactments, the British naturally became furious with the Pande family.

As it seemed difficult to make the Thapa group any stronger and more powerful so long as Karbir Pande and Kulraj Pande remained in power, Sherjung, with the consent of the queen, hatched a conspiracy to remove them from their positions. A complaint letter, largely based on fictitious material, was filed with the palace on 30 October 1842, stating that 'Fattejung Shah, Ranganath Poudel and Prabhu Shah are working to split the country into three parts and distribute it among themselves. Correspondence is going on regarding this matter among them; better be careful.' Leaflets carrying this complaint were then pasted on the walls of the various lanes of Kathmandu city. When the author of the letter was traced, it led to a certain Moharsingh Das, who was then duly arrested. When his hand was chopped off on the orders of King Rajendra, Moharsingh fainted and then died shortly after. It was also discovered that somebody who lived at the pilgrim's inn of Bhim-Mukteswor, near Sherjung Thapa's residence, had delivered the letter to the palace. This person, too, was arrested, and on being questioned, he mentioned the name of Kulraj Pande—he had of course been prompted to do so by Sherjung Thapa. So Kulraj, though innocent, found himself under arrest.

King Rajendra and Prime Minister Fattejung Shah failed to understand that all of this was part of a conspiracy. Without making any inquiries, the Pande brothers were put in chains—on their feet and necks—and subjected to daily whippings. Their property as well as that of their elder brother Ranajung Pande, who had become insane, was confiscated, and several officials who had taken their side were jailed. However, even after this incident, the Governor of Palpa, Ranadal Pande, Kulraj's younger brother, continued to carry on in office as no pretext could be found to trap him.

Peace prevailed in the kingdom during the two years of Fattejung Shah's administration. However, Fattejung was increasingly getting annoyed with Crown Prince Surendra, whose attitude was becoming more aggressive and cruel. Following the downfall of the Kala-Pandes, the crown prince's authority had been dented; however, he took no cognizance of this fact. He played various kinds of mischief, mostly for his own amusement and, in the process, courtiers, officials, maids and even commoners became victims of torture. However, the crown prince's reckless behaviour delighted the queen; she thought that this attitude would come in handy towards the fulfilment of her own aspiration, which in this case was to get the throne for her son.

So when the queen proposed that she could easily put restraints on the unruly conduct of the crown prince if she got control of the administration, King Rajendra, fed up with the reckless behaviour of his son, concurred. The proposal also drew the support of Fattejung Shah. Then, as planned by Fattejung, a citizens' group comprising courtiers, officials, religious personalities and the common folk approached the king and lodged a complaint against the conduct of the crown prince; they also requested the monarch that the control of the administration be handed over to the queen. The king, who was essentially a weak-minded person, was incapable of using his conscience to distinguish between right and wrong. So about one month later, on 5 January 1843, as advised by Fattejung Shah, the king handed over to his queen all the authority concerning the administration of the kingdom by affixing the print of his palm on an authorization paper. To put it in a nutshell, the document, called the Palm Paper,* denied the king and the crown prince the power to issue orders directly. It stated that all the directives concerning the administration should henceforth be channelled through the queen. In the eyes of the people, King Rajendra still held the high command, as all official circulars were issued under his name, bearing his red seal; however, for all practical purposes, the king had turned himself into Rajyalaxmi's puppet.

In her bid to take control over the administration, the queen had also won Prime Minister Fattejung over to her side. But she knew quite well that Fattejung would not support her when it came to realizing all her desires, so she wanted some other influential person to replace him as prime minister. Her infatuation with the Thapas still remained—small wonder then that the Thapas received due encouragement. Rajyalaxmi had also already made up her mind to call back Mathbarsingh

---

* Neither the original nor the copy of this paper has been traced yet. But since General Padmajung Rana has narrated this incident in his biography of Jungbahadur Kunwar Rana and since the document also finds mention in Sir W.W. Hunter's biography of Brian Hodgson, there is ground to believe that the incident actually happened.

Thapa, who had fled Nepal three years earlier, and was now living in exile in Shimla, India. Soon after she took control of the administration, she sent her men to Shimla, along with a letter seeking his return. Though the letter bore the stamps of authorization of the king and the crown prince, Mathbar was reluctant to return. Yet, he left from Shimla, arriving at Gorakhpur where he halted, unable to decide whether to enter Nepal or not.

By this time, Jungbahadur Kunwar, Mathbar's nephew, had climbed high up the ladder of power. He was sent to Gorakhpur to convince Mathbar to return to Nepal. Mathbar's dilemma about whether or not to enter Nepal was resolved once his nephew told him that Nepal's obtaining political situation was indeed favourable to him, and that he was being called back so as to be appointed the prime minister of the country—Mathbar was told that the king too supported the idea of his prime ministership. A few days later, on 17 April 1843, Mathbar arrived in Kathmandu in style.

In Kathmandu, Mathbar was accorded a grand welcome. Earlier, a group of courtiers accompanied by a military contingent had been sent out to receive him, at the distance of a night's halt from the capital. Prime Minister Fattejung Shah, as the chief administrator of the kingdom, was also obliged to participate in the welcome ceremony. As for Mathbar himself, smart, shrewd and wealthy as he was, he had brought gifts and presents worth thousands of rupees. With some of these special gifts, he presented himself before the king and the queen.

By this time, Mathbar understood well that he was expected

to play a crucial role in running the affairs of the state. So, he soon began to assert his authority. In Kathmandu, he refused to go to his residence, saying, 'I will not enter the house without washing away the stains of the poison case from the Thapa family.' And so, he camped at a public inn on the outskirts of Kathmandu city. It is said that none of his acquaintances who went to visit him at the camp returned empty-handed—they were all given gifts and presents.

The queen, since she had to realize her own selfish ends, gave in to the arrogant ways of Mathbar. She convinced the king that Mathbar's demand vis-à-vis the poison case was logical and rational. Then, about two and a half months later, a meeting of the Courtiers' Council was convened and a review ordered on the poison case involving the Thapa family. The meeting, attended, among others, by the king and the queen, turned out to be stage-managed; the council went on to absolve the Thapa family of the crime, declaring it innocent. The documents that had been presented earlier as proof of the family's involvement were deemed fake. By winning the case, the Thapas also won back their confiscated property. Moreover, the council pronounced that the Kala-Pandes were the guilty party in the poison case and that they were the ones who had forced Bhimsen Thapa to commit suicide. The members of the Pande family, including Kulraj Pande, Karbir Pande, Ranadal Pande and Dalbahadur Pande as well as Ranabam Thapa had already been imprisoned. Many innocent officers appointed during the administration of Senior Queen Samrajyalaxmi were dismissed from their posts as they were deemed to belong to the anti-Thapa faction.

In this farce enacted in the name of delivering justice, courtiers such as Fattejung Shah, who had all along followed a neutral path without taking either the Thapa or the Pande side, were forced to lend their support to the verdict that favoured the Thapas. King Rajendra and the courtiers present on the occasion expressed their support to the verdict by affixing their personal stamps on the verdict paper prepared on Mathbar's directive. Thus, on 13 July 1843, the Thapas were given a clean chit.

Generally speaking, the Kala-Pandes had all along opposed the idea of conspiracy and murder. As for Bhimsen Thapa, his attempted suicide had to do with the weakness of his own mind, for which nobody else could be blamed. Now, under the pretext of giving a punishment equal to the crime, ex-minister Ranajung Pande, who had been bedridden because of insanity, was paraded in the lanes of the city with a tonsured head before being poisoned to death, on the orders of Mathbar. Kanaksingh Mahat, who had prepared the document, was charged with writing out a confession that had never been made, and was hanged, while Bodhman Karki had his nose and ears chopped off. That very day, all anti-Thapa ex-courtiers such as Karbir Pande, Ranadal Pande, Kulraj Pande, Ranabam Thapa and Kanaksingh Basnet as well as their family members were hacked to death at the cremation ground nearby. Even two-year-old toddlers of these families were not spared. When the male members of the families met with such a fate, what must have become of the females? One can only guess.

Jungbahadur's cousin Devibahadur Kunwar, who was perceived to be on the side of the Pandes, was also victimized.

Jungbahadur, Mathbar's nephew, did his best to save him, but to no avail. Then, Kulchandra Shah, who had already been blinded, was driven out into the hills, while Guru Krishnaraj Mishra was sent into exile. Dalbahadur Pande, Bhimsen Thapa's son-in-law, was able to save his life, but did not go unpunished—his nose was pierced and a ring inserted in it, so as to deride him as unmanly; he was also dismissed from his job. During this time, many had to flee their country, while many others were maimed or imprisoned; many also had their heads tonsured. And all of these people lost their property to confiscation.

Queen Rajyalaxmi was carrying out all these actions based on the advice of Mathbarsingh. As her sole intent was to weaken the positions of King Rajendra and Crown Prince Surendra, she must have taken delight in the fact that almost all the nobles and courtiers belonging to the camps of the king and the prince were being wiped out. Also delighted was Mathbar on taking revenge on the enemies of his father's elder brother. Only after wreaking this revenge did he move to his old mansion, which had now been released to him.

Bhimsen Thapa had no sons. But on the death of his third brother Nayansingh Thapa in the Kangada War, he had adopted Nayansingh's two sons, Bajirsingh Thapa and Mathbarsingh Thapa. As Bajirsingh died young, his son Sherjung had grown up as a grandson in Bhimsen's residence. As for Mathbar, who had looked upon Bhimsen as his father, he had been appointed an army captain when he was sixteen. By the end of Bhimsen's tenure as the chief administrator, Mathbar had climbed to the post of 'junior general'. Likewise,

Sherjung's first appointment, too, had come when he was sixteen—as a 'commander general'.

Handsome and physically well built, the affable Mathbarsingh Thapa had endeared himself to many nobles and courtiers. But he also smacked of arrogance, a trait that enraged a few other courtiers. For him, the Kala-Pandes were the arch enemies. Mathbar had also become a wealthy man, having bamboozled Bhimsen Thapa in order to wrest significant stakes from contracts in east Nepal. This also explains his display of wealth while living in exile in Shimla.

Surreptitiously, by this time, the Nepalese royal palace had been split into three different groups. King Rajendra obviously wanted to run the administration himself, keeping both the queen and the crown prince under his control. Queen Rajyalaxmi was most anxious to make her son Ranendra the king by casting aside both King Rajendra and Crown Prince Surendra. For his part, Surendra, who had already been declared the heir apparent, had started mounting pressure on the king to hand the state authority over to him. And each of these three factions was only too eager to woo Mathbar, whose support was now considered vital for any plan to succeed. Mathbar himself was least concerned about the feuding among the royal family. Fully satisfied with the devastating crushing of his rivals, he was only concerned about realizing his ambition, which was to reach the pinnacle of power. Queen Rajyalaxmi was extremely eager to elevate him to the post of prime minister, whereby her own ambition could be realized. In the end, the queen held sway and, with her support, Mathbarsingh Thapa took unto himself the ultimate authority of the Kingdom of

Nepal under the title of Minister and Commander-in-Chief, on 18 December 1843.

The title granted Mathbar the authority to defy, citing national interest, the orders of even the king and the queen. He was now authorized to not only hold the high positions of prime minister and commander-in-chief, but beyond that he could be the unchallenged autocrat of the kingdom. Under this new arrangement, Fattejung Shah, a loyalist of the king, was demoted by one grade to the position of an ordinary minister, while Captain Gagansingh Bhandari, who belonged to the queen's camp, was promoted to the position of a senior official and inducted into the new council of ministers. Henceforth, all these nobles and courtiers were supposed to follow the command and directives of Mathbar.

Fattejung, however, could not swallow the insult, and left the country for India, camping at Gorakhpur, where he was reportedly held up by an illness. In response to his escape, Fattejung was charged with arrears of Rs 12 lakh; his house was then confiscated. (Not long after, his brother Guruprasad Shah and son Khadgabikram Shah joined him in Gorakhpur.)

Soon after the assumption of power by Mathbarsingh, the British appointed Major Henry Laurence as their Resident in Nepal, replacing B.H. Hodgson. This unexpected change of envoy sent shivers down the spine of the queen who feared that her scheme might not work out ultimately.

By this time, only three states, namely Nepal, Punjab and Gwalior, remained independent states in the Indian subcontinent. But British interference was felt in the internal administration of all these three states. In the case of Nepal, the British had lent their support to the return of Mathbarsingh to Kathmandu, so as to put Nepal's internal affairs in disarray. It seemed that the British governor general, Ellenborough, planned to seize Nepal's sovereignty and independence through interference. Hodgson had been perceived to be too weak a person to accomplish this task. Hence came his replacement.

Less than a month after Mathbarsingh assumed power, the British invaded Gwalior and established their authority over the state. This news came as a shock to the Nepalese king, queen and courtiers. Moreover, during this time, disorder was prevailing in the general administration of Nepal. The military, too, was in a state of disarray, with its officer corps consisting mostly of unqualified and untrained people whose recruitment had to do with favouritism and nepotism. The passes and routes in the different corners of the country were in a state of near dilapidation. Besides, no arrangement as such was in place to collect and deploy arms and ammunition. Under these circumstances, the king as well as his subjects felt that, in the event of an attack by the British, Nepal would easily lose its independence and sovereignty. By this time, the recruitment of Nepalese youth into the British Army of India had already begun. So, if there was any hurdle in the plan of the governor general, it was the 'Gurkha' soldiers. However, at this time, possibly in July 1844, Lord Harding replaced Ellenborough as the governor general, and Nepal could steer itself through what was considered to be a difficult time.

Meanwhile, desirous of a speedy implementation of her plan, Queen Rajyalaxmi had confided in Mathbarsingh Thapa.

And although he was not prepared to help the queen with this scheme, he gave her verbal assurances of help in order not to disappoint her. Aware of the fact that the king, the queen and the crown prince were powerful in their own ways, Mathbar did not want to antagonize any one of them. So, he spent his first year of administration raising the military's strength and strengthening his own hold on national politics. He successfully shifted to his command the military battalions that had earlier been placed under the commands of Fattejung Shah and other courtiers.

Thanks to this enlarged military strength, now neither the king nor the queen could do anything to restrain Mathbar. He continued giving verbal assurances to the queen about helping her son ascend the throne, but also began inciting Crown Prince Surendra against the king and the queen so that Surendra could get the authority to rule. It was largely on Mathbar's provocation that Surendra declared: 'Along with the throne, I am entitled to the authority to rule, currently vested in the queen mother.' A tussle between the king and the crown prince ensued, and on the advice of Mathbar, the fifteen-year-old crown prince first went over to Bhaktapur to make it his home, and later descended to the Terai. In the meantime, Fattejung Shah had left Gorakhpur for Gaya in India.

Mathbar had encouraged the crown prince to head towards the Terai as part of a plan under which power would be wrested from the king and the queen after confining them to a secluded place. Saying that 'if the crown prince moves beyond the territories of the Nepalese kingdom, it will amount to breaking the agreement with the British, and infuriate them', Mathbar sent both the king and the queen to the Terai, apparently to cajole the crown prince to return. Then, accompanied by a large army battalion, Mathbar, too, followed the royals. The king and the queen arrived at Hetauda, close on the heels of the crown prince. At a secluded corner of Hetauda, now known as Dhukuwabas, both the king and the queen were detained, amid a huge military presence. The king then affixed his handprint on a document that sought to transfer authority to the crown prince (in this document, Surendra was referred to as Baby-King). Thus, on 25 November 1844, Mathbar succeeded in handing over the entire authority to rule the Kingdom of Nepal to the young Crown Prince Surendrabikram Shah.

It is said that, reacting to Mathbar's proposal to hand over the authority to Surendra, the king had at first hit Mathbar with his baton. But the king was flabbergasted when Mathbar scolded him saying that he might end up confined inside a room at the palace. So, he was literally forced to affix his handprint on the document prepared on Mathbar's orders. Queen Rajyalaxmi had remained a mute spectator to this episode. However, a few courtiers did protest at this daredevil act. Indeed, an elderly military officer was hanged to death at the very site for registering his protest, and eighteen soldiers were beheaded in an apparent bid to quell the protest against Mathbar.

Now Mathbar did not give two hoots about the king or the queen. Almost leaving them in the lurch, he returned to Kathmandu immediately along with the Baby-King. Surendra was accorded a festive welcome in the capital. Close on Mathbar's heels, the king and the queen also surfaced in

Kathmandu; however, there were no front-riders or welcome ceremony for them.

But while Crown Prince Surendra might have assumed full control over the administration, the fact was that he was quite an inexperienced and inefficient ruler. So, Mathbarsingh established himself as the de facto ruler. And thanks to his enlarged military strength, the ministers were also rendered almost powerless. A few days after returning from Hetauda, Mathbar ordered the pajani function, wherein he dismissed main courtiers like Ranganath Pandit and Abhimansingh Rana—all belonging to the king's camp. Gagansingh Bhandari (Khawas) was stripped of his ministership though his position as guardian of a junior prince remained undisturbed. Also dismissed from service was Fattejung who was at that time on a pilgrimage to India—he was charged with the punishable crime of stepping into British domains; so he remained in Gaya. His property was then confiscated. All of Fattejung's brothers and nephews were also removed from their posts. Another dismissed courtier, Abhimansingh Rana, fled to Gorakhpur. While some nobles and courtiers did receive reappointments, their retention was in name alone—all the troops under their command were shifted to the command of Mathbarsingh.

Now some nine thousand troops served under Mathbar's command. He appointed his son Ranoujjwal Thapa as the 'commanding colonel'; Ranoujjwal also headed the entire army under Mathbar's command. The military strength that Mathbar mustered helped him raise his power and authority to the level once enjoyed by his father's elder brother, Bhimsen

Thapa. Now there was no one who would dare challenge his authority. In the first four months of his rule, he also received three awards, each with a purse of one lakh rupees. But as he built up the nation's military, besides introducing reforms in the administration, British Resident Henry Laurence started growing suspicious of Mathbar.

As Mathbar gave special importance to Crown Prince Surendra, leaving both the king and the queen to fend for themselves, the royal palace at Hanumandhoka had turned into a venue of disgruntled nobles and courtiers, who would make adverse comments on Mathbar's activities. On one occasion, Mathbar even refused to meet the king when he arrived at the prime minister's residence; this obviously made King Rajendra furious. And no less infuriated with Mathbar was the queen, who felt that he had betrayed her, scuttling all her plans and programmes. So, the queen was now determined to destroy Mathbar, even if it meant wooing the king over to her faction. But because of the huge military backing that he enjoyed, the queen knew that arresting Mathbar would not be as easy as it had been in the case of Bhimsen Thapa—only a conspiracy could decimate him.

Soon after he had returned from exile, Mathbar had obtained from the king a promise as a royal grant; it had said: 'You will not be murdered.' These words were inscribed on a tiny copper plate, which Mathbar called the 'amulet of immortality' and wore around his neck. From the king, he had also obtained a special sword, which he called the 'sword of immortality'. Mathbar carried the unsheathed sword with him all the time. He felt fortified by this 'life-giving ammunition'.

In his conversation with the British envoy Henry Laurence, he once reportedly said: 'From the time of Prithvinarayan Shah till today, almost all prime ministers of Nepal have met with untimely deaths. But I am going to be the exception.' But as he uttered those words, little did Mathbar realize that his days too were numbered.

During the time of King Prithvinarayan Shah's rule, Sirdar Ramkrishna Kunwar had emerged as a courtier as well as a brigade commander of repute. His eldest son, Ranajit Kunwar, had three sons. Of the three, the eldest, Balnarsingh Kunwar, had been appointed a courtier when Bhimsen Thapa ran the administration. For his second marriage, Balnarsingh had taken Mathbarsingh's younger sister as his bride, and from that alliance, Jungbahadur Kunwar Kshettry was born in the year 1817. Although he was illiterate, Jungbahadur was rich in practical knowledge. Apart from being highly skilled in the use of arms and ammunition, he was very proficient in swimming, horse-riding and hunting, including elephant-chases. Cheerful and affable, he endeared himself to the ordinary folk, and was quite smart when it came to winning friends. At a young age, he had cultivated qualities that would take him a long way in his march towards success. During Bhimsen Thapa's downfall, Jungbahadur had just stepped into adulthood. Naturally, he did not remain unaffected by the fall. So, while young, he had been forced to put up with all kinds of troubles and difficulties. In those distressful times, he had developed an addiction towards smoking hashish, and even gambling. Later, Jungbahadur got into a familial relationship with Prasadsingh Basnet, who had found a berth in the then council of ministers, by marrying Prasadsingh's daughter for his third wife. Courtesy this relationship, Jungbahadur started off as an ordinary administrative servant; he then made a steady progress up the ladder of success, making it to the position of the bodyguard of the crown prince. Later, after his maternal uncle Mathbar rose to prominence, Jungbahadur is found to have succeeded in elevating himself to the position of kazi within a period of three years.

Jungbahadur Kunwar had lent a helping hand to Queen Rajyalaxmi when she wanted to bring back Mathbar from exile in India. Actually, Jungbahadur seems to have endeared himself to all the three factions. His elevation to the high post of kazi had the support of Mathbar who wanted him as a close confidant. He was also entrusted with the task of keeping in touch with British Resident Henry Laurence; meanwhile, his brother Bambahadur Kunwar was appointed the Nepalese envoy in Calcutta. Seemingly, Jungbahadur also organized the hunting expeditions of the British Resident. Close ties with the Resident enabled Jungbahadur to read the mind of the British government.

However, when his maternal uncle Mathbar enacted a law that prohibited any courtier, except the prime minister, from taking command of more than three hundred soldiers, Jungbahadur started nursing a grudge against him. Under this ruling, the troops under his command were also withdrawn. Mathbar, however, seemed to be unaware of Jungbahadur's resentment towards him.

About two years earlier, Devibahadur Kunwar, son of Jungbahadur's uncle, had been charged with treason, and it had been almost certain that he would be given capital punishment. Jungbahadur had made a strong plea to Mathbar to save Devibahadur's life. And had Mathbar so wanted, Devibahadur could have been saved; but that had not been the case. Consequently, Devibahadur had been put to death. Now Jungbahadur was even more furious with Mathbar though the latter remained unaware of it. No doubt, Mathbar had risen to become the all-powerful autocrat of the Kingdom of Nepal by dint of his own personality, grit and courage, but by this time, he also smacked of arrogance, much to the disenchantment of even the nobles and courtiers close to him. Now he had only his two sons and a couple of orderlies left as his true well-wishers. Until this time, Gagansingh Bhandari had remained as a counsellor to the queen. He carried a lot of clout at the royal palace. Meanwhile, Mathbar had dismissed Kulmansingh Basnet, a courtier loyal to the king. Yet Kulmansingh, a brother of Prasadsingh Basnet's and therefore by relation an in-law of Jungbahadur's, was a frequent visitor to the royal palace.

So, as advised by Gagansingh Bhandari and Kulmansingh, Queen Rajyalaxmi started hatching a conspiracy against Mathbar. As the participation of Jungbahadur was deemed vital to the plan, a proposition was made to him through Kulmansingh. The proposition placed Jungbahadur in a quandary. He knew quite well that his maternal uncle Mathbar, largely because of his conceited behaviour, was heading towards doom, and it was something that might even take place shortly; and Jungbahadur was also certain about his own downfall should Mathbar meet his doom. At the same time, he also knew that he would not have any chance of further success in his life as long as Mathbar remained in power. So, driven by this selfish motive, and with utter disregard for the right or wrong of things, Jungbahadur swore his participation in the conspiracy being hatched against Mathbar.

As a part of the conspiracy, a decision was made to call Mathbarsingh Thapa to the royal palace on the night of 17 May 1845. Accordingly, around 9 p.m., Mathbar was summoned to the palace via an urgent message from King Rajendra. The message read: 'The queen is gravely ill; she may not survive; we have to take her out to the ghat; please come immediately.' But when Mathbar did not arrive at the palace after receiving the royal message, Kulmansingh Basnet rushed to Mathbar's residence around 10 p.m. Now Mathbar could no longer ignore the royal message.

It is said that on that night, Mathbar's mother, Ranakumari, had advised him, saying, 'Because it is night-time, you don't go alone, [go] only with reliable associates.' But full of conceit that no one would dare try anything against him, he ignored his mother's advice. His bodyguards, too, were equally suspicious, suggesting that he should go only after daybreak the next day. 'Don't come if you are afraid; I will go alone,' a visibly irritated and annoyed Mathbar shot back to his seniormost bodyguard. Downstairs, on his way to the palace, he tried to mount his horse, which, however, was reluctant to give him a ride. But Mathbar would not yield, firm as he was in his trust in the inscription and the unsheathed sword of immortality. He arrived at the royal palace on foot around 11 p.m., dragging his horse behind him. He was accompanied in his journey by Kulmansingh Basnet.

On the terrace of the ground floor of the Hanumandhoka Royal Palace, King Rajendra reclined on an ornate bed, while the queen, supposedly gravely ill, lay on a bed inside the adjoining room. At one end of the queen's room Jungbahadur Kunwar lay waiting, shielded by a curtain. At another corner, in order to assist him, stood Gagansingh Bhandari on full alert. No sooner had Mathbarsingh Thapa sat down on the chair nearby, after paying his respects to the king and sheathing his sword of immortality, than two powerful bullets hit his chest and head. The bullets fired from behind the curtain felled the forty-seven-year-old Mathbar. Before long, the influential general understood that he had become the victim of treachery. Stretching out his folded hands, he piteously begged the king: 'Let my old mother and orphaned children be protected.'

But the king who had earlier obliged Mathbar by presenting him with 'tokens of immortality' was now furious with the man who was begging for pity and mercy. Showering him with all kinds of verbal abuse, King Rajendra brutally struck Mathbar's trembling arms with his kukri. Mathbarsingh Thapa died shortly thereafter, and his body was set on fire before dawn.

While this tragic incident was taking place at the palace, Mathbarsingh's sons were awaiting their father's return to their mansion, where they were playing a game of dice. Now, as if to tell them that he was not a party to the murder, Jungbahadur sent out a message to Mathbar's sons, asking them to 'immediately escape to a foreign land, before dawn'. And the young sons, who did not dare to act in revenge, and who thought that their best bet lay in saving whatever property they owned, dashed out of the valley that very night. Jungbahadur's brother Runodeepsingh Kunwar, who had carried the message, helped Mathbar's sons reach the border. The female members of Mathbar's family escaped the next day, carrying with them the gold and ornaments left behind by the sons; left behind was only Mathbar's immovable property, which then was duly confiscated.

The next day, King Rajendra gave a recount of all the crimes that Mathbarsingh had committed; then he proclaimed: 'I myself killed him by shooting and striking him with the kukri.' That same day, all the nobles and courtiers who had been sacked by Mathbarsingh Thapa were reinstated to their respective positions. Yet, some fears still lurked in the mind of the king that perhaps the troops supporting Mathbar would revolt. So, all the administrative offices were ordered to be closed for ten days, and security was beefed up with special arrangements in the royal palace as well as the whole capital.

Soon after the incident, on 1 June 1845, in accordance with her promise, Queen Rajyalaxmi rewarded Jungbahadur by giving him charge of the state treasury, along with the command of three regiments of soldiers. King Rajendra concurred with the queen's decision. The couple, although driven by different personal motives, were both delighted at the removal of Mathbar from the scene. However, even as the two of them attempted to woo and win over Jungbahadur to their respective sides, Jungbahadur remained focused on his own aggrandizement.

No matter what the king had said in his declaration about the death of Mathbarsingh Thapa, no one believed that King Rajendra himself had actually wielded the gun. Everyone thought that it was Gagansingh Bhandari who had pulled the trigger. And even when some of them pointed the finger of suspicion at Jungbahadur, it was dismissed, as no one believed that he could open fire at his own uncle. So for two years, complete secrecy was maintained about the fact that Jungbahadur had been a party to the conspiracy and that it was he who had pulled the trigger. During this period, none of the conspirators dared to reveal the secret; nor was it considered necessary. The mystery behind the betrayal of Mathbarsingh Thapa would unfold only after the Kot Massacre incident.

Unpublished, written probably in 1961

Six

The Kot Massacre and the Dawn of the Rana Rule

Following the demise of General Mathbarsingh Thapa, the Nepalese royal family faced the crucial question of who would take control of the country's administration. While King Rajendra wanted to keep it to himself, Queen Rajyalaxmi had hatched the conspiracy against Mathbar driven by her desire to wrest the all-important authority. From a legal standpoint, both the king and the queen had bequeathed the authority to Crown Prince Surendra when he was invested with the title of Baby-King. It was indeed a complicated issue, since neither of them was prepared to see their powers rescinded.

Also confused was the nobility, which however quickly worked out a formula. A 'peace plan' aimed at maintaining peace and harmony among the king, the queen and the crown prince was made. Accordingly, on matters of state administration, the king would direct orders to the crown prince, who would then pass them on to the queen, while the queen would in turn relay them to the courtiers. When the courtiers placed this modus operandi before the trio, all the claimants to the authority agreed. Thus, acquiring the documents and papers duly stamped by both the father and the son, Queen Rajyalaxmi again assumed control of the state administration, on 26 May 1845.

Even though the queen had taken full control of the administration, the king, being the source of all orders and directives, had not lost his say in matters. Yet, since the queen had the right to the red seal, no important decisions that would go against her wishes could be taken. But because all directives originated from the monarch, there was a kind of joint control over the administration. In this division of power, practically speaking, the crown prince turned out to be the loser since his authority was now wedged between that of the king and the queen.

When the new Courtiers' Council was being formed, the queen expressed her desire to appoint Gagansingh Bhandari, loyal to her son Ranendrabikram Shah, as prime minister. King Rajendra's choice for the position was Fattejung Shah. In the end, the king prevailed, and Gagansingh had to settle for the position of acting prime minister and commander-in-chief only for the year's rainy season. During this time, Ranganath Pandit and brother Krishna Pandit were living in exile in India, just like Fattejung Shah and Abhimansingh Rana. Now the Pandit brothers' allocations were restored and released though they had not yet returned to Kathmandu. Fattejung and Abhimansingh returned to the capital in September, thereby speeding up the formation of the new council of ministers.

In the new Cabinet, Fattejung Shah was appointed the prime minister, courtesy the king. He was also given the charge of three regiments as well as the passes and routes of west Nepal. The foreign affairs portfolio also belonged to him. Fattejung got back the property that had been confiscated by Mathbarsingh Thapa. Abhimansingh Rana was inducted into the council of ministers and given the charge of two regiments as well as the administration of east Nepal. Dalbhanjan Pande also joined the council of ministers, holding the charge of one regiment. These three ministers were said to belong to the king's camp. Jungbahadur Kunwar, who had earlier made it to the rank of army general, and who had been in command of three regiments, was reinstated to his post under the new dispensation. On the strong recommendation of the queen, Gagansingh Bhandari was taken into the council of ministers and given the charge of seven regiments. The capital's military arsenal and the administration of Kathmandu valley were placed under his command. By virtue of the vast authority vested in him, Gagansingh became the de facto prime minister, while Fattejung remained one in name alone.

Gagansingh now became the closest and most trusted confidant of Queen Rajyalaxmi. Confident that she could fulfil her ambition with his help, she revived her old plan of forcing King Rajendra to abdicate so that her son Ranendrabikram could be placed on the throne. She had long coveted the position of regent so that she could have a monopoly over state affairs. Around this period, however, Nepal's military organization was almost in a shambles, much to the delight of the British envoy, Major Henry Laurence.

Now two factions, one headed by the king and the other by the queen, had surfaced on Nepal's political landscape; but

Crown Prince Surendra had been rendered nearly powerless. Military officers dominated the council of ministers, now clearly split into two groups, and the tussle for power was intense. And each faction took for granted Jungbahadur's support. But Jungbahadur himself, although he maintained contact with both the factions, was driven by his own aspirations. Both King Rajendra and his wife, blinded as they were by selfish motives, were unable to see that a situation was being created wherein they would not only be sidelined but could also possibly become the victims of an unanticipated disaster.

As is often expressed, whoever is sly, courageous and ambitious, and whoever can sail with the winds taking cognizance of the changed times, ultimately emerges the victor in any power struggle. Viewed from this standpoint, Fattejung Shah and his brothers, who belonged to the faction headed by King Rajendra, and who had lived a life of comfort and luxury throughout, were ill-prepared to make sacrifices when called upon to do so in crucial moments. Gagansingh Bhandari, belonging to the queen's camp, had become old and was devoid of the guts or courage required to undertake adventures. So, clearly, the tussle was between Abhimansingh Rana, the king's man, and Jungbahadur Kunwar, the queen's. Both were young, shrewd and energetic. But they were poles apart in one respect: while Abhimansingh was all by himself, Jungbahadur had six of his brothers by his side, always prepared to 'do or die' during crucial times. So destiny was on Jungbahadur's side, a fact that had remained beyond the grasp of the king and the queen.

At the time these political events were taking place in Nepal, in India, the British were making preparations for an invasion of the Sikh state of Punjab. Governor General Harding called Resident Laurence back from Nepal, as he was a military officer who had spent a long time in Punjab and was familiar with the conditions prevailing there. (For almost one year, the position of the British Resident in Nepal was kept vacant, until Major Thoresby was sent in December 1846.)

Now, all of a sudden, the Nepalese royal palace received a letter from the Punjab state, requesting assistance against the British. The letter put Nepal in a predicament: in case of a war, who should Nepal support—the Sikh camp or the British forces? When the issue came up for protracted debate in the council of ministers, all the three ministers belonging to the king's side pleaded for helping the Sikh side, while Gagansingh Bhandari and Jungbahadur Kunwar, supposedly the queen's men, argued that Nepal's assistance should go to the British. So, no reply was given to the letter of the Sikh state; instead, a letter was forwarded to the British governor general stating that Nepal was desirous of sending its troops as requested by the British. It was also decided that Jungbahadur would take command of the Nepalese troops in the event of Nepal going ahead with aiding the British.

King Rajendra and the courtiers on his side were keeping a close watch on the Anglo-Sikh war. Having concluded that the British would eventually win the war, they came round to the view that if some Nepalese troops could be sent in to assist the British, Nepal could expect the return of its lost territories in Kumaon and Garhwal as a reward. However, the British achieved complete victory over Punjab even before Nepal's letter expressing her desire to send troops reached them. So, the king's hopes were belied. Now the British Resident in Kathmandu also began to become more assertive.

Meanwhile, the queen had begun to disregard the monarch, and was interfering in the discharge of responsibilities by the courtiers loyal to the king. Gagansingh, the queen's close confidant, assumed full command over the nation's military and its arms and ammunition. Thus, a situation prevailed wherein all the king's men felt suppressed. As the queen wanted to take control over the administration by doing away with all the king's men, she clearly knew that Gagansingh Bhandari would be of invaluable assistance to her in this undertaking. She also left no stone unturned to secure the support of Jungbahadur. On his part, Jungbahadur was keeping a close watch on the moves of the ministers and courtiers of both the factions; he was assessing their strength and mental capability. In fact, he was waiting for an opportune moment when he would be able to bring about the downfall of both the factions so that he could emerge as the unchallenged ruler of Nepal.

By this time, Jungbahadur's six younger brothers and various other relatives had formed themselves into a viable and strong group. One of his brothers, Bambahadur, had been promoted to the position of a minister, and he was in charge of the treasury office of Kumarichowk. This time, Jung, too, seems to have put in some efforts in firming up the military establishment; in the process, he had appointed his other brothers to the captain and lieutenant ranks of the army. As for his other relatives, his uncle's son Bakhtajung Kunwar and brother-in law Sanaksingh Tandon were very close to him. At least nine others who were in regiments under his command had turned themselves into loyalists and were part of the famous Band of Eighteen Brothers. These eighteen brothers, all below thirty, were of a fiery temperament, ever prepared to do or die.

At this time, a young and ambitious Brahmin named Bijayaraj Pande surfaced on the Nepalese political scene. A storyteller by profession, he first entered the household of Gagansingh Bhandari as a preceptor who gave sermons to Gagansingh's two sons; later, he made his way to the royal palace as a storyteller and reader of religious books for Queen Rajyalaxmi.

Here it has to be mentioned that while Gagansingh was unflinchingly loyal to the queen, and the queen, too, trusted him fully, she had found it difficult to converse with Gagansingh within the walls of the palace on matters that were prejudiced against the king. So, in a secluded room inside the palace, set aside for worship and other sacred rituals, she would meet Bijayaraj and, through him, send Gagansingh messages concerning political matters. Jungbahadur knew of the liaison between the queen and Bijayaraj, and he chose to use it for his personal gain, particularly to get to know of the goings-on between the queen and Gagansingh. In the process, Bijayaraj and Jungbahadur became thick friends, leading the former to eventually join Jungbahadur's faction.

However, even as these tie-ups were being forged, there erupted on the Nepalese political theatre a volcano of great proportions. On 14 September 1846, around 10 p.m., a bullet unexpectedly pierced through the body of Gagansingh while he was deep in prayer in the first-floor room of his house—he died instantaneously. He was possibly shot from the roof of his house.

Later, Gagansingh's neighbour, Lal Jha, was identified as the person who had shot him, but this was not known at the time. Lal was said to be an aggressive young man. Gagansingh had once sent him to serve as the orderly of Prince Ranendra, the son of Queen Rajyalaxmi. When Gagansingh had been building his new house, after being appointed as minister, he had acquired and demolished the neighbourhood settlement of the Udas community, and there had also been a plan to demolish more houses to have more space for the corridor and the courtyard of his mansion. In the process, a quarrel had taken place between Gagansingh and the Jha Brahmins, leading to the dismissal of Lal Jha from the service of Prince Ranendra. Out of this rancour, it seems, Lal Jha had decided to kill Gagansingh.

Now questions arise: Was Lal Jha alone in the deed or did somebody prompt him to do it by supplying him with the gun and bullets? One version being bandied about since that very time is that 'Jungbahadur himself had in disguise shot Gagansingh to death'. Also repeated is the version that Jungbahadur had assigned his brother Badrinarsingh to do the job. But doubt could be cast over all these versions, especially because Lal Jha vanished after Gagansingh's assassination. The events that had unfolded that night immediately after the murder do suggest that Jungbahadur was an accomplice and it was he who had given Lal Jha the ammunition. Jungbahadur's calculations for the moment were: if Gagansingh could be killed clandestinely, all blame would go to the faction led by Fattejung Shah, at least in the queen's eyes. Based on the accusation, all courtiers loyal to the king, including Fattejung, could be sidelined, thus paving the way for Jungbahadur to become prime minister. And, even if the premiership were to be beyond his grasp, he would certainly attain the position of commander-in-chief held by Gagansingh. Perhaps, this is all he had expected at that time.

The Courtiers' Council met at Sishmahal (Glass Mansion), a newly built edifice close to the royal palace. Bhimsen Thapa had built it with glass windows. The venue for the meeting was the mansion's hall at its eastern end; the ground-floor rooms of this elegant mansion housed military hardware, and it was famously known as Kampu-Kot. Kot was also the name given to the courtyard south of the mansion. It was here in this courtyard some three years before that Kala-Pandes like Ranadal Pande and Karbir Pande, ringed by some 500 soldiers, were bashed up black and blue, with King Rajendra and Prime Minister Fattejung Shah supervising the operation.

Sishmahal was about five minutes' walk north-west from the Basantapur Royal Palace; at an equal distance stood the mansion of Gagansingh. So, in no time, the news of his assassination reached the palace. The murder of her closest confidant left Queen Rajyalaxmi stunned and infuriated. Carrying an unsheathed sword and accompanied by maids who carried lit torches, she stormed into Gagansingh's prayer room. The sight of Gagansingh's lifeless body lying in a pool of blood incensed her even more. Before leaving the room, the queen thundered out a stern order saying that the body was not to be cremated 'until the killing is avenged by counter killings'. Then she arrived at Sishmahal, an investigation into the murder clearly on her mind.

At Sishmahal, she issued an order for the bugle to be blown from atop the Dharahara so as to urgently assemble the nobles, courtiers and military officers. And, as if he was the one person who knew about everything in advance, the sly Jungbahadur reached there before the bugle was played. At the sight of Jungbahadur, there was some dilly-dallying in transmitting the queen's order to play the bugle, with the result that there was some delay in its playing. It seemed that Jungbahadur wanted to ensure that he had made all the preparations before the other nobles and courtiers poured in.

Jungbahadur had surely known exactly when or at what time Gagansingh would be gunned down. That was why, pretending to be unaware of the developments and making it look as though he were dedicating more time to look after the royals, Jungbahadur had stayed back on the palace grounds till ten on the night of the murder, monitoring from there the goings-on at Gagansingh's residence. Some 500 soldiers were stationed at Chhauni Barrack just outside Kathmandu city, under the command of Jungbahadur's brothers, and they had been directed to 'report as soon as a signal is received'. So, soon after receiving Jungbahadur's message, and even before the bugle blew, the soldiers of Chhauni Barrack were seen scurrying around to encircle the Kot and the corridors of Sishmahal.

The queen had unwittingly placed herself in a precarious

position. If the bugle had been blown promptly, she might have been better off, but because of the delay, she had already been outplayed, although she did not realize it. If she had so wanted, she could have had people assembled within a quarter of an hour by sending messengers on foot to call them. The courtyard would have been filled with her courtiers and Gagansingh's soldiers. The houses of Fattejung Shah and Dalbhanjan Pande were closer to Sishmahal than Jungbahadur's residence at Thapathali. General Abhimansingh Rana's residence stood at about five minutes' walk from the royal palace. It never occurred to the queen that these people who belonged to the king's side would do her any harm—another vital mistake. These were the things that might have made her situation very different, but unfortunately, destiny had something else altogether in store for the queen. She had counted rather excessively on Jungbahadur for support.

At Sishmahal, the queen did ask why the soldiers were encircling the Kot compound. But it was not a difficult task for somebody as cunning as Jungbahadur to immediately come up with an explanation. He replied that all these arrangements had been made to ensure the safety and security of the queen. Even at that time, the queen believed that it was Fattejung Shah and other courtiers belonging to the king's side who had conspired to murder Gagansingh. Her sycophants at the court had been filling her ears for a long time, saying that Birkeshar Pande was an opponent not only of Gagansingh's but also the queen herself, which was why she suspected Birkeshar's hand in the murder, and was breathing fire at him. Lending credence to her suspicion was the fact that Birkeshar was still active as the special attendant of Crown Prince Surendra. The queen shared this thought with Jungbahadur, who was standing by her side. He replied that he was in complete agreement with her assessment, and told her repeatedly that she was wholly correct on the matter.

Jungbahadur was not one to miss such an opportunity arising out of the queen's grief. He had completed his preparations; he counselled the queen that she should immediately assemble all the courtiers, adding that she should first put Birkeshar Pande in chains and then have him whipped so that he would confess to the murder and also reveal the names of all those who were involved with him in the heinous act. He further advised the queen to behead Birkeshar only after he confessed to the crime and to imprison or punish in some way all the courtiers named as accomplices in the murder. Blinded as she was by her selfish motive of placing her son Ranendra on the throne so that she could grab power as the regent, Queen Rajyalaxmi failed to comprehend Jungbahadur's sneaky calculations. She readily accepted his suggestions; and in a show of reaffirming his trust in him, she named him commander-in-chief, handing over the authority it entailed.

Now, in the Kot courtyard, Jungbahadur was the principal performer. He knew that he would never again get such an opportunity to settle scores with his enemies. He had already deputed about a dozen members of his band to invite only those courtiers who held regiment commands, leaving out those denied the command. And of those who held commands, Jungbahadur's close relatives were uninvited. For Birkeshar's arraignment proceedings, bamboo poles were erected for him to be tied to, while whips were kept ready. Shackles and chains were requested from the adjoining courtroom. Kalu Shahi and Singhbir Pande were the first ones to arrive at the Kot. Both were arrested with no questions asked.

Abhimansingh Rana's residence was close to Gagansingh's. He had heard about the murder almost immediately and, in his heart of hearts, he knew the perpetrator was Jungbahadur. And when Jungbahadur's men came to his house to call him, his suspicion was reinforced. After he heard that two courtiers had been arrested on entering the Kot, Abhimansingh was completely convinced that Jungbahadur was the mastermind behind the whole plot. The alert man that he was, Abhimansingh, accompanied by some 200 soldiers who were living in rented houses in his neighbourhood, reported straight to the Hanumandhoka Royal Palace, taking a detour around the Kot. Before leaving home for the palace, he had also advised the same route for Dalbhanjan Pande. So at around 11 p.m., Birkeshar Pande and his three brothers arrived at the royal palace, accompanied by Abhimansingh Rana, Dalbhanjan Pande and others.

At the royal palace, King Rajendra was in an indifferent mood, quite unmoved by the news of the assassination of Gagansingh. The queen did not seem to care for the monarch. It was in such a situation that Abhimansingh Rana and other courtiers dashed to the palace. In their conversation with the king, they spoke about the likelihood of some joint action that might be taken by the queen and Jungbahadur in response to the murder of Gagansingh. A disaster was imminent, the king was told. They proposed that the royals, including Crown

Prince Surendra, confine themselves to the palace all night and visit the Kot only after daybreak the next day. But a timorous King Rajendra declined the proposal, fearing that his absence would trigger a reprimand from his wife—he decided to go to the Kot right away. This decision stunned Abhimansingh and his fellow courtiers, but for want of an alternative, they were forced to quietly follow the king. Jungbahadur had already deputed his men at the royal palace. One of them was Bijayaraj Pande who had been specifically instructed to not let the king out of the royal palace, even if that involved using threats and force. Jungbahadur had perhaps rightly thought that the monarch's presence in person at the Kot would prove to be detrimental to his own plan as it would raise the morale of the king's courtiers, and embolden them. When King Rajendra began to leave the palace, Bijayaraj stopped him, saying: 'Do not go there; your personal safety is in danger.' For a while, he tried to hold the king back, but then Abhimansingh Rana intervened and asked Bijayaraj to back off.

Jungbahadur had issued strict orders to the army officers to allow only those into the Kot courtyard who had been invited and to stop the others. Jungbahadur's eighteen brothers knew who had been called, and King Rajendra was certainly not one of them. Yet, when the king came, no one dared to stop him; thus, the monarch, along with his bodyguards, gatemen and other attendants, made his way into the Kot compound— against Jungbahadur's orders. Likewise, some uninvited army officers managed to sneak in, along with Abhimansingh Rana and Dalbhanjan Pande.

While King Rajendra was entering the Kot courtyard,

Queen Rajyalaxmi and General Jungbahadur were standing at the foot of the steps leading towards Sishmahal. Seeing Birkeshar Pande alongside the king, the queen, her eyes all red with fury, demanded: 'Show me the murderer of my minister.' Then turning to Abhimansingh Rana, she pointed her finger at Birkeshar Pande and said: 'He is the one; cut him down, right now.'

The queen's words left Abhimansingh aghast. He raised his eyes towards the king, who had now been rendered fearful and nervous by the angry posturing of his wife. Yet, in an attempt to mollify the queen, he said, 'The issue is very intricate; we cannot cut somebody down just for the heck of it. Fattejung Shah, too, has not arrived yet. We will find out who the murderer is after he arrives and then do whatever is necessary. Wait a while.'

The king's words were received in silence all around, with the queen too staying quiet for a while. In the meantime, more invitees came in.

However, unfortunately for the king, even as they waited, Fattejung Shah did not show up. Then, saying that he himself would bring him, King Rajendra left the Kot grounds, making his way towards Fattejung's residence at Narayanhity. But when he stepped out, the soldiers who had encircled the Kot allowed only the monarch to leave. Acting on Jungbahadur's signal, the soldiers held up the king's attendants and even his bodyguards, preventing them from following their monarch. It is reported that when the king arrived at the residence of Fattejung 'in the darkness of midnight', he was in a pitiable condition.

Before the king's arrival, Jungbahadur's brother Bambahadur

Kunwar had already reached Fattejung's residence in order to call him to the Kot. On his part, Fattejung had called his brothers and relatives such as Naraharibikram Shah and Dakshya Shah, to his mansion, and a debate had ensued on whether the journey to the Kot at night was advisable. All had expressed their views though the final decision was yet to be taken. On his arrival, the king, addressing all of them, said: 'The situation at the Kot will not calm down until you all go there; let us go.'

Then Fattejung Shah, citing the intricate situation that prevailed at the Kot, submitted to the king: 'We may return from the Kot safely only if we take the British envoy along with us; otherwise, we might fall into the ambush of Junge.' Adjudging the minster's suggestion to be right, King Rajendra said: 'In that case, you all keep going. I will bring the envoy.' He then left for the British residency at Lajimpat in the darkness of the night.

Here it has to be said that destiny did not seem to be in favour of the king during this time. Though he held the top command of the nation, the monarch himself was passing through a pathetic stage in his life. There had been a time when the nobles and courtiers waited in line at the palace, their hands folded, for favours and orders from the king, but now he was the one knocking the doors of his courtiers, seeking their help and assistance.

That night, King Rajendra somehow made it to the gates of the British residency, throwing all diplomatic protocols to the wind. But at the gate, the king was told that the acting Resident 'does not see people at night'. Thus, the master of the nation was turned back by a junior officer at the behest of the envoy. A disappointed and disheartened King Rajendra returned home. While returning, he avoided the Kot courtyard and went directly to his palace. Avoiding the Kot, however, turned out to be the greatest blunder of his life—visiting it before entering the palace could have dramatically altered the situation.

Meanwhile, Fattejung and his team had moved slowly, expecting the king and the envoy to catch up with them before they reached their destination. Even so, they arrived at the Kot in almost no time. When Fattejung and his men entered the courtyard, Jungbahadur's soldiers denied entry to their armed bodyguards. The queen was at Sishmahal, her eyes riveted on the path by which Fattejung Shah would arrive, while Jungbahadur stood by her side, feigning an attempt to console her grief. As soon as Fattejung entered the courtyard from the main entrance, Jungbahadur got down the steps and pretended to offer a salute. Then, moving closer, he whispered to Fattejung, apprising him of the details of all that had happened, along with the fact that the queen was mad with anger over the loss of Gagansingh. Apparently, so as to read Fattejung's mind, Jungbahadur even said, 'Whatever you say, I will follow. I am even ready to arrest the queen.' While Fattejung and Jungbahadur conversed quietly, the queen stepped down the stairs of Sishmahal and rather unexpectedly pounced upon Birkeshar Pande, saying: 'I will cut you down myself.' Fattejung Shah, Abhiman Rana and Jungbahadur intervened to hold the queen back, and all agreed to arrest and question Birkeshar in order to find out the truth behind the murder, and initiate action against him, if needed. Birkeshar was immediately arrested but no charge was brought against him. When he was questioned, Birkeshar gave all possible clarifications. Yet the queen remained unconvinced; so to placate her, Birkeshar was put in shackles. The time now was 1:30 a.m., the same time around which King Rajendra was returning to his palace, circumventing the Kot courtyard.

With the shackling of Birkeshar, the queen's anger was pacified to a certain extent and she returned to the hall, climbing back up the stairs. All this while, Jungbahadur acted as the closest confidant of the queen. Carrying lit candles, he led the way for the queen to reach the sitting room, while Fattejung Shah, Abhimansingh Rana and Dalbhanjan Pande stood at the foot of the stairs, hoping that the queen would summon them. But no sooner had the queen entered the sitting room than gunfire burst out all of a sudden—all the three ministers were shot from behind, with the bullets passing through their bodies.

As it was a night of the dark moon, no one could see where the bullets had come from or who had opened fire. Fattejung and Dalbhanjan fell immediately, while Abhimansingh, who was shot in the leg, forced himself to hobble away. The courtiers and others present in the courtyard remained unaware of the shooting. Actually, it was Ranamehar Adhikari, Ramu Ale and Bhim Ale, all members of the famous Band of Eighteen Brothers, who had opened fire simultaneously on a signal from Jungbahadur. The injured Abhimansingh limped away to the western end of the courtyard where the courtiers belonging to the Fattejung camp stood chatting. Pointing to his blood-soaked leg, he said, 'Junge got General Gagansingh murdered at his house; he has taken the lives of Fattejung and Dalabhanjan here; I have been treated this way; what are you all waiting for?"

Abhimansingh's appeal for help was indeed overwhelming, and this stirred up Fattejung's brothers and sons against their rivals in the Jungbahadur camp. But as Abhimansingh was trying to exit the gate, dragging his injured leg, watchman Judhabir Adhikari impaled him with his bayonet, taking his life there and then.

Small wonder that the news of the atrocious killings at the Kot did not reach King Rajendra immediately. Jerked awake from his bed by the delayed message of the killings, King Rajendra tried to rush towards the Kot. But Bijayaraj, who had been assigned at the palace to keep surveillance on the king, blocked his path at the main gate. He told the king: 'That place is rife with violence; you should not go there; the bastards can do physical harm to you too.' That simpleton that he was, the king believed Bijayaraj and, instead of rushing to the Kot courtyard where he could possibly have rescued many of his loyal supporters, King Rajendra drew himself back to the warmth of his bed at the palace.

In those days, whenever nobles and courtiers were summoned, they carried their swords with them. Accordingly, most of the courtiers assembled at the Kot that night had their swords with them. However, Jungbahadur and his brothers were not only carrying swords but also guns and bullets. Also present on the scene was Fattejung's son Khadgabikram Shah, an energetic young man of twenty-one. When he found out about his father's murder and realized who was responsible, he unsheathed his sword from his waist and, like a wounded tiger, pounced on Jungbahadur's brothers. The darkness of the night prevented him from recognizing even those people who were standing close to him. However, the darkness was also rendering ineffective the guns and bullets of Jungbahadur and his brothers, as it was fraught with danger to open fire in the melee. But, despite being surrounded from all sides by Jungbahadur's brothers, Khadgabikram waged a lone battle. That was when, somehow Jungbahadur faintly saw the plight of his brothers and, sensing disaster for them, opened fire from the sitting room of the Sishmahal, felling Khadgabikram. Meanwhile, Birbahadur Shah, Khadgabikram's uncle, also wielded his sword against the Jung brothers for some time, but was soon killed.

Now no one was left at the Kot who would be able to stand up against Jungbahadur and his band. All of King Rajendra's men who were still alive were trying to save their own lives. There was no way a group carrying swords could successfully battle a group wielding guns. So Jungbahadur, his brothers and other followers seized and killed one by one many of the courtiers, bodyguards, watchmen and attendants belonging to King Rajendra's side. A few of them managed to escape by climbing the compound wall, while some others fled through the drainage pipes. There were also some from the king's camp who were able to escape by virtue of being Jungbahadur's relatives; indeed, Jungbahadur's brothers aided their escape.

One of the escapees was Kulmansingh Basnet, believed to be one of the king's associates. He was stabbed on his shoulder with a kukri by one of Jungbahadur's men. He then fell on the heap of dead bodies and, remaining still, feigned death. After calm returned, he rose to his feet and left the place quietly.

It was around 2 a.m.—on the ninth day of the dark moon— when tranquillity returned to the Kot courtyard. Both Queen Rajyalaxmi and Jungbahadur spent the rest of the night at Sishmahal, protected by their soldiers.

Despite his crucial role in the atrocious massacre, the queen still regarded Jungbahadur as her closest confidant. Now she wanted to scare off Crown Prince Surendra, a permanent thorn in her side; so, before returning to her palace at daybreak, she ordered Jungbahadur 'to show in detail the entire scene of the massacre to the crown prince'. While Jungbahadur was not in a position to promptly dismiss the queen's order, he also did not want to create terror in the mind of the crown prince by showing him the horrendous scene at the Kot. In fact, he had designed the entire operation so that he would be able to wrest full control over the affairs of the state by placing the crown prince in the front, sidelining both the king and the queen. As dawn broke, he woke the seventeen-year-old Surendra, who was sleeping in his room, and carried him on his back to the massacre site. Then, as he narrated the whole sequence of events to the crown prince, he downplayed both the incidents leading to the carnage as well as the bloodletting itself by portraying them as natural and commonplace.

The funeral rites of the courtiers killed at the Kot began only after this display to the crown prince. Now, as Jungbahadur and his brothers feared that the nobles and courtiers who had managed to escape last night would revolt and assemble their soldiers, a declaration was made to the effect that all the courtiers who had fled the Kot the previous night should cross the Charbhanjyang (four points of exit out of the Kathmandu valley) before sundown the next day, and if they failed to do so, they would be 'cut down on the spot'. One of the escapees, Kulmansingh Basnet, was spotted early in the morning, but as he was a relative of Jungbahadur's, his wounds were dressed up, and Jungbahadur took him into his group.

When he had orchestrated the massacre, Jungbahadur had feared none except the British. However, he had already convinced the acting British Resident Captain Oakley that he was a friend of the British. So the British chose to gloss over the Kot killings; moreover, they did not see any adverse reaction to the incident. For a long time, British envoys in Nepal had been apprising Governor General Harding that Jungbahadur was on their side, unlike Fattejung Shah who belonged to the king's camp. So, as far as the events of that fateful night at the Kot were concerned, Oakley took delight in what was perceived to be the rise of the group that supported him and the liquidation of the group that opposed him. The governor general had been tight-lipped when informed about the incident. It seems Jungbahadur had read the minds of the British well before planning the move against the king and the queen.

In the annals of Nepalese history, the night that witnessed the horrendous killings in the Kot courtyard is famous by the name of Kot Parba. Following is the roster of those who died, those who fled the scene, and those who were banished in the aftermath of the carnage:

Those who were killed included:
Fattejung Shah, Khadgabikram Shah, Naraharibikram Shah, Abhimansingh Rana, Dalbhanjan Pande, Ranajor Thapa, Narsingh Thapa, Goprasad Shah, Dalbahadur Shah, Bakhtabahadursingh Bhandari, Birkeshar Pande, Kirtidhoj Pande, Samarbahadur Shah, Gunaprakash Shah, Satrubhanjan Shahi, Yuddharanjan Shahi, ArjunThapa, Capt. Mohanbir Shahi, Capt. Narsingh Shahi and his son, Capt. Birbahadur Shah, one person known only as the son of Badriban Shahi, Gaida Malla, Dada Dandakeshar, Jogram (gatekeeper), Bishnu Bhagat, Kalu Khawas and Indrabir Raut.

Those who escaped:
Narayan Pandit, Hemnath Pandit, Dakshya Shah, Babarjung Shah, Singhabir Pande, Kalu Shahi, Dalkeshar Pande, Birbikram Shah, Narayansingh Thapa, Sumedsingh Kunwar, Jayadrath Adhikari, Ranakeshar Shah, Dada Rassingh, Capt. Kulchandra Rana, Capt. Ratnasingh Rana, Purnachandra Shahi, Capt. Jayabikram Shah, Singhadal Gurung, Kesharsingh Raut, Bhuminandan Upadhyaya, Bikramarka Malla, Gopi Pandit, Raghunath Dhungana, Raghubir Basnet, Bhotu Thapa and Juddhabir Rana.

Those who were banished:
The entire family of Mathbarsingh Thapa, family of Ranabirsingh Thapa, families of Jangabir Pande and Tribikram Thapa, family of Sherjung Thapa, family of Santabir Thapa, and family of Bhabanibhakta Shahi;

individuals: Chautariya Jyan Shah, Chautariya Kodandajit
Shah, Capt. Bhairabbahadur Pande, Capt. Kirtibir Thapa,
Capt. Bhaktikumar Hamal, Shaktibir Hamal, Faudasingh
Kunwar, Abhinsingh Khatri, Gyannidhi Upadhyaya, Ajaya
Singh, Debu Upadhyaya, Sahadutta Pandit, Trilochan
Upadhyaya, Kashinath Upadhyaya, Sarbajit Thapa, Mushi
Dhai, Juddhabir Raut, a cousin of Dadhiram Upadhyaya,
and Ratnabadan (gatekeeper).

Two persons, namely Khadananda Upadhyaya and
Ranganath Khanal, and a third one, known only by his
surname Kuikel, had their heads tonsured on four sides as
punishment.

The Kot carnage occurred around the midnight of a
Monday. The sentences of tonsure and banishment were
carried out the next day. Those who had fled the scene hurried
out of the valley on Tuesday. Guruprasad Shah and Tribikram
Thapa (who had been in jail) went into exile from Palpa, while
Bhimbikram Shah made his way to India from Doti.

Thus, Jungbahadur became Nepal's undisputed despot,
removing the nobility of King Rajendra's camp from the
political theatre of the kingdom once and for all. Neither
the king nor the queen could do anything by way of taming
him. Crown Prince Surendra had become a puppet in
Jungbahadur's hands. Two days after the massacre at the
Kot, Jungbahadur formally assumed the positions of prime
minister and commander-in-chief. His brothers Bambahadur
Kunwar, Badrinarsingh Kunwar and Jayabahadur Kunwar were
respectively given the charge of the treasury office, auditor's

office and the department of administration; another brother, Krishnabahadur Kunwar, was appointed the administrator of Palpa district, while three other brothers became colonels in the army.

But it was not just about their posts and positions—Jungbahadur and his brothers became the rulers of Nepal. The destiny of Nepal and the Nepalese lay in their hands. The massacre at the Kot had laid, if it can be so described, the foundation for the Mansion of Rana Rule in Nepal.

Unpublished, written in 1961 under the title 'Establishment of Rana Rule through Violent Revolution'

Seven

The Bhandarkhal Episode and the Internment of Queen Rajyalaxmi

King Rajendra received a sketchy account of the Kot bloodbath the very night it occurred. Grief-stricken by the shocking loss of many of his loyal courtiers, the monarch spent the night fuming and fretting and reflecting on his future that looked bleak indeed. All the while the day was breaking. By this time, the queen, too, had returned to the palace from Sishmahal, but she had not encountered the king as yet. So the king did not exactly know what had led to the massacre, or why so many nobles and courtiers had been slain, all at one go.

Meanwhile, at dawn, General Jungbahadur arrived at the palace, ostensibly to pay his respects to the king, but he presented himself in the manner of an army commander who had just won a battle. The previous night at the Kot, he had obtained unofficially from the queen the title of 'commander-in-chief'. Small wonder then that the king was almost frightened when Jungbahadur appeared in full regalia. The king knew that Jungbahadur was the mastermind behind the previous night's gathering of the nobility at the Kot courtyard.

Now he assumed that Jungbahadur was the main person behind the conspiracy too and that the queen had perpetrated the massacre possibly on his advice. On seeing Jungbahadur, who had unexpectedly appeared in the commander-in-chief's uniform, a visibly agitated king asked, 'Who ordered the massacre of so many courtiers? What wrong had they done?'

However, Jungbahadur was in no mood to yield to the king, as now all his rivals among the powerful and influential courtiers had been exterminated, and as he had won the full support of the queen. Moreover, he held command over enough regiments. So, he replied nonchalantly, 'All this happened on the orders of the queen whom you have vested with all the powers; I am innocent in all this.'

Jungbahadur's firm and fearless reply was indeed provocative, and the king, roused to anger, ran towards the queen's room. The queen was still infuriated over the murder of Gagansingh, and had failed to comprehend Jungbahadur's scheme. King Rajendra repeated to her the question he had asked Jungbahadur. Scornful, the queen replied, 'Not much has happened until now; more is yet to come—you better watch out.' The queen's annoyance stemmed from the monarch's refusal to withdraw the special rights bequeathed to Crown Prince Surendra. What was more, suspicion still lingered in her mind that the king and his loyalists had been behind the murder of Gagansingh.

Her harsh reply sent the king into a frenzy of anger. In reality, during that time, both the king and the queen were, so to say, standing on a narrow precipice, and the best course for them would have been to mend their fences and cooperate with each other. But the queen remained blinded by her selfish motive, while the king would not tolerate derogatory words from his wife. As already stated, while King Rajendra's future looked bleak, he also faced the challenge of conducting himself in accordance with the changed reality. There was nobody he could look to for advice. Almost at his wits' end, the thirty-four-year-old monarch unexpectedly walked out of the palace, saying, 'It is meaningless for me to stay here; I will go into exile, in Kashi.' Outside the palace, he picked up Sirdar Bhabanisingh Khatri for company, before heading to Bungmati in Patan.

Queen Rajyalaxmi still fully trusted Jungbahadur. Her dream of making her son Ranendrabikram Shah the heir apparent and, if possible, even the king by removing Crown Prince Surendra and his brother Upendrabikram remained intact. However, she was unaware of the fact that Jungbahadur had clandestinely made a deal with both the crown prince and his brother.

In a bid to convince the queen of his unflinching loyalty, Jungbahadur enacted a drama wherein the crown prince and his brother were interned at the royal palace. The reality, however, was different: Jungbahadur stated to the crown prince and his brother that if ever they schemed against the queen, he would support them. So the crown prince and his brother also looked upon Jungbahadur as their paramount well-wisher and saviour, as well as one who would shield them from the queen's assaults.

King Rajendra was caught in the crossfire of the altercation between his wife and son, as his character inherently lacked the capacity to take decisions. The Kot killings had occurred largely because of the king's irresolute mind and the queen's unbridled ambition. Following the killings, Jungbahadur hung like the proverbial sword of Damocles over both their heads. The problem that occupied King Rajendra's mind then became how to run the administration by reining in Jungbahadur on the one hand and removing the limitless power vested with the queen on the other. On his way to Patan, he halted at Tundikhel (the parade ground) where he probably discussed these issues with Sirdar Bhabanisingh Khatri. Jungbahadur, for one, was on the lookout for excuses. From his intelligence sources, he received news of the king holding discussions with his friend, and this he quickly reported to the queen in a rather exaggerated form. The news incensed the queen, who had by this time become quite wayward in her ways. In a fit of anger, the queen then issued an order 'to immediately behead Sirdar Bhabanisingh and present his head before me'.

On the queen's orders and Jungbahadur's directive, a trusted soldier named Kaladhar beheaded Sirdar Bhabanisingh while he lay asleep at night. The next morning, Bhabanisingh's head, blood still dripping from it, was presented to the queen at the royal palace. An innocent courtier was brutally killed right under his nose, yet the king could do nothing but watch silently. The beheading of Bhabanisingh hurt King Rajendra's feelings terribly. He was now indeed in a predicament: what should he do? Then, on 16 September 1846, Jungbahadur had the king brought back to the royal palace, sending his brother Runodeepsingh Kunwar to fetch him.

On the third day since the Kot Massacre, the queen officially vested Jangbahadur with the office of commander-in-chief.

The same day an official announcement was made to the effect that he had also been appointed prime minister. And that very day, Jungbahadur took the salute of honour for both the positions at a military parade held in Tundikhel. King Rajendra was forced to give his consent to these decisions.

By orchestrating the Kot Massacre, Jungbahadur was also attempting to malign the royals in the eyes of the common people, while projecting himself as the only honest person around. In the first place, the queen was portrayed as the perpetrator of the bloodbath. At the same time, Jungbahadur had taken steps to keep the king and the queen under effective control, while pledging undying support to Crown Prince Surendra. The queen, who had by now become completely wilful, still did not comprehend the fact that Jungbahadur's intentions were wicked; she continued to believe that he was her admirer and was obedient to her.

By this time, the festival of Dasain was approaching and it was also time for the annual pajani of military and civil servants. Putting up the queen as a front, Jungbahadur carried out the year's pajani, of course in the manner that suited him best. As many nobles and courtiers had recently died and many others had been dismissed from service, there was no dearth of vacancies. Jungbahadur succeeded in promoting each of his brothers and other trusted loyalists by at least one grade. This helped him amass more powers. Now that all the regiments of the kingdom were under his command and as all his rivals had been removed from the political scene, Jungbahadur attained a position from where he could conveniently ignore the orders and commands of both the king and the queen.

Time flew. Queen Rajyalaxmi was becoming increasingly anxious about implementing her plan of suppressing her step-sons Crown Prince Surendra and his brother Upendrabikram Shah. At a time when he had not yet strengthened his hold on power and influence, Jungbahadur had sounded vaguely positive about the queen's plan. All along, he had been advising the queen to stay patient and wait until the king's consent came and when ways could be found to circumvent public criticism. But now, the queen discerned that Jungbahadur was strengthening his own hold on power by the day, and was paying scant attention to the execution of her plan. One day she summoned all her courage to once again remind Jungbahadur of her wish to have her son Ranendra as the heir apparent. This time, too, Jungbahadur turned a deaf ear to the queen's proposition. He had already made a general assessment that the queen was trying to seize power only because of the king's feeble-mindedness and that both the military and the general populace were actually fed up with the couple's conduct; he arrived at the conclusion that the king and the queen could no longer pose any danger to him personally.

Gradually it dawned on the queen that Jungbahadur's assistance would not be forthcoming in realizing her aspirations. She began to regret all that she had done in the recent past—all of which had to do with her reposing full trust in Jungbahadur. Now she chose to forget her plan of action and instead began contemplating an intrigue against Jungbahadur. But alas! She had by this time lost almost all the courtiers who, because of their loyalty to her family, could have helped her in this time of need. Most of them were now dead, and the few who had managed to survive had gone into exile. Now taking the few remaining loyalists into her confidence, the queen began hatching a conspiracy against Jungbahadur—she even won King Rajendra's consent to it in the end.

It was as clear as daylight that the murder of Gagansingh Bhandari had been the handiwork of Jungbahadur. While Gagansingh's sons and the few courtiers who were loyal to the king were furious with the prime minister over that act, thus far they had remained silent for fear that by speaking out against Jungbahadur, they would only antagonize the queen. Meanwhile, Pandit Bijayaraj Pande continued to hold his sway at the royal palace. He had been specially appointed by Jungbahadur to monitor the daily activities of the king and the queen—something else the queen unfortunately remained unaware of. Though infuriated with Jungbahadur, the queen regarded Bijayaraj as one of her trusted confidants. For his part, Bijayaraj, who spent most of his time at the royal palace feigning loyalty towards the royals, was Jungbahadur's informer. It was in these circumstances that the queen was plotting the arrest and dismissal of Jungbahadur.

Kazi Birdhoj Basnet and Captain Vajirsingh Bhandari, Gagansingh's son, had come forward as the queen's main accomplices in this undertaking. It is said that at this time Birdhoj was assured that he would get the office of the prime minister in the event of the successful execution of the queen's plan. Vajirsingh, who was furious with Jungbahadur over the murder of his father, saw in this assurance a brighter future for himself. Dalmardan Thapa, too, was roped in as an accomplice. The queen then decided that Bijayaraj Pande should also participate in the conspiracy, and accordingly, he was taken into confidence. But Bijayaraj promptly alerted Jungbahadur about the plot.

One day, pretending that an urgent errand needed attention, the queen sent for Jungbahadur, asking him to 'immediately report to the royal palace'. The queen's plan was to forcibly arrest him and strip him of his positions of the prime minister and the commander-in-chief. The incident involving the subduing of Mathbarsingh Thapa, the erstwhile prime minister and commander-in-chief, about one and a half years before, flashed in her mind. But the existing political and social conditions were different from those that had prevailed one and a half years earlier. While at that time, Mathbarsingh had been all by himself, now Jungbahadur had six brothers by his side, ever ready to 'do or die'. Moreover, there were many other loyalists who remained alert and careful on his behalf. Jungbahadur had also won over the confidence of the British government in India. The queen failed miserably at taking note of this obtaining reality. She wrongly presumed that power would flow smoothly into her hands once Jungbahadur was detained.

Of all people, the queen sent Bijayaraj to bring Jungbahadur to the royal palace. He had already informed Jungbahadur of all the suspicious activities taking place in the palace. Arriving at Jungbahadur's residence, Bijayaraj told him that the invitation from the royal palace could possibly be a part of the queen's plot against him. The crafty Jungbahadur did not want to let this opportunity pass without extracting some benefit from it. He was determined to keep for himself the offices of the prime minister and the commander-in-chief; not only that, he wanted these positions for his descendants for generations to come.

Responding to the call from the palace, Jungbahadur left his residence, accompanied by his brothers and other close aides, fully armed. Meanwhile, when Jungbahadur did not promptly arrive at the palace, the queen dispatched Birdhoj Basnet to bring him. At a short distance from the palace, near the present-day Jorganesh Temple, Birdhoj bumped into Jungbahadur's armed group. On Jungbahadur's orders, Ranamehar Adhikari slaughtered Birdhoj then and there.

Inside the royal palace compound, at the Bhandarkhal Garden, some officers and soldiers loyal to the queen were lying in wait for their enemies. Jungbahadur and his group stumbled upon these men who were still awaiting the queen's command to act. They were indeed frightened by the aggressive posturing of Jungbahadur and his band. No sooner had he arrived at the garden than Jungbahadur proclaimed that whoever laid their weapons down would 'only be imprisoned', while those who refused to do so would be beheaded.

Accordingly, those who laid down their arms were arrested, while those who were reluctant to do so were summarily slaughtered. In this incident, altogether twenty-three persons were cut down, while many more were cast into jail. Captain Vajirsingh Bhandari and Dalmardan Thapa somehow managed to escape the assault; both fled the country later.

The queen had been closely watching the happenings of the day. The news of the killings and arrests of her close courtiers involved in her plan dumbfounded her. Now Jungbahadur, accompanied by his band, rushed to the palace and, on his orders, the queen was interned immediately. The king remained a silent spectator.

A couple of days later, as a reward for helping Jungbahadur, Bijayaraj Pande was appointed as the royal preceptor, while his elder brother Tirtharaj was offered the position of the chief priest at the royal palace.

Following the internment of the queen, King Rajendra lost whatever little confidence he had; a couple of days later, he was making preparations to go into exile in Kashi along with the queen. By then, the king was under Jungbahadur's thumb. Thus, in a letter addressed to Jungbahadur, and with his red seal affixed, the king proclaimed: 'Henceforth, all the regiments and courtiers should take orders from Jungbahadur Kunwar. I will go to live in Kashi [in exile]; should Queen Rajyalaxmi and her sons try to come back, that should not be allowed; if they decide to fight, you can hit back.'

Not long after, Jungbahadur produced another red-seal letter approved by the king; this was addressed to Crown Prince Surendrabikram, and it said: 'I am going to Kashi; you place yourself on the throne in the event of my arrest there; otherwise, you ascend the throne after I complete forty years of age.'

Thus, following the Bhandarkhal incident, both the king and the queen were forced to toe Jungbahadur's line, while Crown Prince Surendra had already become a puppet in his hands. All in all, Jungbahadur Kunwar succeeded in becoming Nepal's absolute ruler.

The violent incident that occurred at the garden of the Hanumandhoka Royal Palace on 31 October 1846 is known as the Bhandarkhal Episode in the annals of Nepalese history.

Unpublished, written in the year 1960

Eight

The Alou Episode and the House Arrest of King Rajendrabikram Shah

Following the Bhandarkhal Episode, Queen Rajyalaxmi, stripped of all her authority, was reduced to a cipher. An order of banishment was served to her, stating that she was no longer entitled to remain at the royal palace. On the day it was issued, she was moved to an ordinary house at Makhantole and interned there. The very same person upon whom she had heavily relied to realize her ambitions and to whom she had lent all her support throughout had now become her detractor numero uno. And none of her well-wishers and elderly courtiers had survived. With no respite in sight, Queen Rajyalaxmi was now forced to express a wish to go on a pilgrimage to Kashi. Her minor sons, princes Ranendrabikram Shah and Birendrabikram Shah, agreed to join her on the pilgrimage. Naturally, Jungbahadur welcomed the queen's proposal.

In the changed context, the ill-fated King Rajendra, too, grew more vulnerable by the day. He found it almost inconceivable that he would be staying alone at the royal palace, while his wife would be in exile. He, too, had lost all his advisers and followers one by one and he had ceased to trust Jungbahadur and his brothers. Greatly disillusioned by the Kot Massacre, the king yearned for some peace of mind and he assumed he might attain it by going on a pilgrimage, howsoever brief. So when the issue of the queen leaving for a pilgrimage came up, the king, too, was prepared to accompany her. Jungbahadur did his best to dissuade the king and hold him back, but he stuck to his guns for once. Jungbahadur was then forced to give consent to the king's departure.

On the advice of Jungbahadur, King Rajendra appointed Crown Prince Surendra as the regent, stating in an authorizing letter that the latter run the affairs of the state until his return from the pilgrimage. 'In the event of my arrest, you should occupy the throne,' the monarch said to his son in the letter. Subsequently, on 23 November 1846, the king, accompanied by some of his family members, departed for Kashi. However, before the king's departure, Jungbahadur put forth a condition that said the monarch should return home within three months, failing which Crown Prince Surendra would officially assume all the authority of the state.

Preparations began to be made for the king and queen's pilgrimage. The officials and bodyguards who were to take care of the royals were appointed. A couple of Jungbahadur's trusted agents sneaked in as bodyguards. The state treasury was to bear all the expenses of the pilgrimage. Jung also gave his men strict orders to try to persuade the king to return home in time. Specially assigned to the job were Captain Karbir Khatri, Captain Khadgabahadur Rana and Subba Siddhiman Singh.

Crown Prince Surendra, who had now acquired the authority once vested with the queen, was indeed grateful to Jungbahadur. He was fully confident that it was Jung who would save him from the malice of the queen. In a way, Surendra had become a puppet in Jungbahadur's hands. The crown prince's official duties were confined to affixing the red seal on documents prepared on the orders of Jungbahadur.

In the Indian religious town of Kashi, the news of the king's arrival spread, and all courtiers belonging to the families of the Shahs, Thapas, Pandes, etc.—all those who had either been driven out from Nepal or those who had fled the kingdom—gathered to meet the king. All the 'refugees' who assembled there had one and only one woe: they had all suffered at the hands of Jungbahadur. For a few days, the queen remained forlorn and dejected, but soon she had her confidence restored, largely because she now had the king with her and because the exiled courtiers regularly offered her words of encouragement. Now she began to incite the king to take revenge upon Jungbahadur, who she believed could yet be crushed. Initially, the king seemed to be indifferent, fed up as he was with what he perceived as dirty politics; however, because of the daily urging of the exiled courtiers and the regular prodding of his wife, he now made up his mind to rise against Jungbahadur. Meanwhile, the officials whom Jungbahadur had assigned to keep a close watch on the royals were regularly sending updates to him about the activities of the king and the queen.

It was Chautariya Guruprasad Shah who was heading the group of exiled nobles and courtiers inciting the royals to take steps against Jungbahadur and his brothers. Fire raged inside

Guruprasad Shah to seek reprisal against the brutal slaying of his elder brother Fattejung Shah and many of his cousins in the Kot Massacre. Actively assisting him in his campaign against Jungbahadur were exiled courtiers like Ranganath Poudel, Bhimbikram Shah, Singhbir Pande, Tribikram Thapa and Kalu Shahi. They were working overtime to devise ways of returning home and suppressing Jungbahadur and his brothers. In the process, several plans were conceived, and also discarded. But there was consensus on one point: the king himself should assume control over the country's administration; and the others would pitch in from their respective positions. The queen, too, gave her consent to the idea rather quickly.

All of them were pinning their dreams on the king. The courtiers told him that if 'Swami Maharaja' Ranabahadur Shah could take successful control over the administration of Nepal after returning from Kashi, there was no reason why King Rajendra couldn't do the same. After plenty of exchanges between the king and these courtiers, it was decided that the king would return to Kathmandu and mount a campaign against Jungbahadur if required. All of them unanimously agreed that before returning, it was essential to build military strength which included the recruitment and training of troops. The queen agreed to bear the expenses that would be involved in this venture.

Time slipped by, and the period of three months that had been stipulated for the king to return from Kashi was nearing its end. While on the one hand, the 'refugee' courtiers wanted their various demands—like advance restoration of their rights—to be met right away; on the other, the monarch was apprehensive that if he failed to meet the deadline to return, Jungbahadur would surely make his life difficult in Kathmandu. Indeed, Jungbahadur had been writing regularly from Kathmandu on behalf of Crown Prince Surendra, pleading with the king to return home as soon as possible. Finally, the king made up his mind to return within the stipulated time and departed from Benaras. The queen and her sons stayed behind.

By mid-February, King Rajendra arrived at the town of Sugauli in India, which lies at a short distance from the Alou village of Nepal. There he again began to debate within himself whether to return to Kathmandu or not. It was largely his fear of Jungbahadur that had prompted him to make his way to Kathmandu. He resented the prime minister, even hated him. The motivations of the queen and the exiled courtiers urging him to return to Nepal weighed heavily on his mind. But he also felt pain and anguish at being compelled to return home, leaving his queen behind in a foreign land. So at Sugauli his legs seemingly began to totter, refusing to move towards Nepal.

Jungbahadur and his brothers knew quite well that the king's men from across the border were clandestinely building up a military force. Jungbahadur's agents, who had been sent to look after the king and the queen, had been regularly apprising him of the daily activities of the royals. So when the king suddenly halted just near the border, Jungbahadur and his brothers were naturally alarmed.

Then Jungbahadur, on behalf of the regent and Crown Prince Surendra, wrote a letter addressed to the king. It said: 'It is vital that you return home immediately; otherwise, it will be deemed a violation of the agreed conditions, and no authority of any kind will be saved for you in the kingdom.' In his reply to the crown prince, the king wrote from Sugauli: 'There should be no ban on bringing back the queen; I will soon return to Kathmandu along with her.' But Jungbahadur was not willing to let the queen return, under any circumstances. He fired off another letter on behalf of the crown prince, which said: 'If you want to return, come immediately, on time; princes Ranendrabikram Shah and Birendrabikram Shah, too, have permission to return to Nepal, but no right can be granted to the queen to step on to Nepalese soil, under any circumstances. It is also vital that you return promptly, otherwise you will lose your authority over the throne.'

Fear and astonishment gripped the king after reading Jungbahadur's sternly worded letter, written on behalf of the regent and Crown Prince Surendra. But he also firmly believed that it would not be right on his part to live in comfort as king in Nepal, while the queen, irrespective of the blunders she had committed, lived in banishment. So, he made up his mind to return to Nepal, not alone and helpless but in the company of a huge following. So from Sugauli, he actively started building up a military force. Courtiers like Guruprasad Shah, Bhimbikram Shah and Dalmardan Thapa, who had already initiated work towards this end, now doubled their efforts. On their part, Jungbahadur and his brothers in Kathmandu were keeping a close watch on all the king's activities at the Indian town.

Communication between King Rajendra and Jungbahadur continued. While the prime minister pleaded for an early return of the king, the latter laid down conditions for the same. This time the main conditions set by the monarch were: he should have the whole authority to carry out the pajani and that he should get the command of all the regiments of the kingdom. The rest of the authority Jungbahadur could keep with himself, so proposed the king. Accordingly, the king dispatched a document of trust outlining these conditions for approval by the prime minister. Jungbahadur, however, declined the conditions and, as the king too stuck to his guns, differences between the two deepened.

Soon, Jungbahadur convened a meeting of the Courtiers' Council in Kathmandu. The assembly passed a resolution in which the courtiers stated: 'Henceforth, we all will follow only the orders of Prime Minister and Commander-in-Chief Jungbahadur; we are unable to carry out your [the king's] orders.' The resolution, clearly aimed at slighting the monarch, was promptly dispatched to him; on reading it, King Rajendra could easily see that efforts were on in Kathmandu to depose him.

In fact, the king found the council's resolution quite distressing. In reply, he wrote an *istihaar-patra* (letter of declaration) addressing the entire Nepalese people, the members of the Courtiers' Council as well as the seventeen regiments of the kingdom. The letter, outlining the prime minister's faults, stated: 'I haven't come here for nothing; I was forced to come here unable to bear the tyranny of Junge; now you have to choose me or him; should you decide to take my side, come up to Katarbana to take me back, as I am willing to return with all of you.

'But I will not return until the authority and rights of Junge are broken down. If you all cannot come here because of malaria, first arrest Junge and his brothers and then come up to Chisapani to fetch me; I will come there along with my courtiers, and we will discuss the matter there.

'In the case of Junge, if he wants justice, he should come to me unarmed and without soldiers; I am willing to give him justice; otherwise, he, too, will be forced to face punishment.'

Two of King Rajendra's trusted agents—Shermardan Hamal and Dambarsingh Bista—were sent to Kathmandu with the declaration letter. They somehow managed to reach Kathmandu, but they had failed to escape the eyes of Jungbahadur's intelligence agents. So no sooner had they arrived in Kathmandu than they were captured. This took place on 11 May 1847. Then the istihaar-patra that bore the red seal of the king was placed before Jungbahadur. The duo had also carried with them a pistol each, meant for their own safety. All along, Jungbahadur had been looking for some ruse to depose the king, and in this incident he found it. In the prevailing political environment, rife with fear and suspicion, it would have been almost impossible for two helpless persons to be able to shoot at someone like Jungbahadur who was ringed by armed guards all the time; nor would anyone have dared to undertake such a dangerous mission based simply on a declaration letter which was not addressed to any particular individual, but to a whole populace. Yet the incident firmed up the prime minister's anger against the king. Jungbahadur's patience was now exhausted as far as waiting for the king's return was concerned.

The next day, another council meeting was convened. At the meeting, attended mostly by Jungbahadur's brothers and his agents, both the men accused of attempted murder were presented, in chains and handcuffs. Then it was unanimously decided to immediately depose the king and appoint Crown Prince Surendra to the throne. The council also agreed to send an intimation letter to this effect to the ex-king as soon as possible. Thus, Crown Prince Surendra was crowned king on 12 May 1847. On the same day, Jungbahadur delivered a long speech at Tundikhel, while Shermardan and Dambarsingh, who had been captured the previous day, were put to death.

The contents of the intimation letter sent to the deposed king Rajendrabikram Shah on behalf of the Courtiers' Council read thus:

Your Majesties' conniving with the Kala-Pandes ended the life of an able minister like General Bhimsen Thapa, and later brought about the downfall of the Pandes by making use of the Thapas. Mathbarsingh Thapa, too, was murdered on Your Majesties' behalf. Likewise, because you handed over to the queen—a woman—all the powers of the state, violating the dignity of the scriptures and the family tradition, horrendous incidents such as the Kot Massacre and the Bhandarkhal killings took place. As if that were not enough, you have now issued a red-sealed proclamation against the prime minister and commander-in-chief. All these acts of yours clearly prove that you are incapable of running the affairs of the state. So, though you were the ruler of this country to date, henceforth we have decided to confer all state authority on Crown Prince

Surendra and place him on the throne as the King of Nepal. Henceforth, you have no rights whatsoever to the throne of the Nepalese kingdom. This letter is aimed at intimating you about our decision. Should you decide to continue living in India, arrangements will be made wherein you will be held in due respect, and appropriate measures will be taken to facilitate your living there. If Your Majesty says you want to return to Nepal, we have no objection; only that, on returning, your status will be that of a deposed monarch . . .

This letter reached the king in no time. And on receiving this piece of astonishing correspondence, he became even more enraged. He was now left with no alternative but to enter Nepal as soon as possible. Accompanied by a large following, he entered the kingdom, camping himself at the Alou village of Parsa district. Jungbahadur still had intelligence men monitoring the king's activities. The king was not prepared to surrender to Jungbahadur immediately. His plan was to make a steady advance towards Kathmandu, but only after equipping himself with some military strength. He now recalled the successful return of his grandfather 'Swami' Ranabahadur Shah. Rajendra also sought assistance from all concerned, including his associates, who were counselling him on the matter of making it to Kathmandu. However, for different reasons, no real aid came forth as the prevailing situation considerably differed from that of the past, but this was something the king failed to comprehend.

At Alou village, as directed by Rajendra, Guruprasad Shah and his associates had been recruiting troops and training them. Now this task picked up pace. Meanwhile, rumours circulated in Kathmandu that Rajendra was now backed by a strong military. Then one night, Jungbahadur dispatched Captain Sanaksingh Tandon and Captain Balabhadra Majhi along with the soldiers of the Purano-Gorakh regiment to Alou with the aim of seizing the king. And as Jungbahadur wanted to show that the newly appointed monarch, Surendra, had joined the group of the ex-king's enemies, he also sent his brother Runodeepsingh Kunwar and King Surendra's brother Upendrabikram Shah, along with an adequate number of soldiers, to Alou. For the deposed king, it was indeed his misfortune that his own son had come to arrest him.

It is said that a letter had been written on behalf of Prince Upendrabikram Shah, which said that if the ex-king left the camp of the 'rebels', he would be taken to Kathmandu 'with honour and dignity'; this letter was then duly dispatched to the deposed king. But Rajendra was determined to move on to Kathmandu in a show of strength. He thought it unnecessary to pay any attention to his son's words. Thus, a fight between the two sides became imminent. However, as Rajendra did not have an effective intelligence and communications network on his side, he failed to receive any information about the troop movement from Kathmandu. Also, he never expected a violent attack against him.

Thus, before dawn broke on 27 July 1847, the trained soldiers of the Purano-Gorakh regiment, led by Captain Sanaksingh Tandon, mounted a surprise attack on the camp of the king's military. The king's 'half-trained' soldiers had been fast asleep when they were attacked. They could not even get hold of their weapons. Thus, nearly one hundred men, including military officers, soldiers and civil servants, were killed; nearly two dozen men were injured and a few arrested. Among the dead were Captain Kirtibir Thapa, Lieutenant Ambar Shahi, Lieutenant Shribhakta Khawas and Subba Kalidas. The remaining soldiers fled in different directions. Battered by this unexpected defeat, the deposed king tried to flee towards Sugauli on elephant back but was captured. Some of his associates, including Guruprasad Shah, managed to escape.

A prisoner now, the deposed king was carried in a palanquin via Makawanpur, and was first brought to Kewalpur en route to Kathmandu. Here, army officers from the high rank of colonel to the low rank of subedar were put on duty, along with cooks, attendants and priests, to attend to the king, and as many as 300 personnel from the Pakhe Company were garrisoned for his security. At Alou, the deposed monarch had enjoyed the company of a woman known as Nani Sahib. Now accused of being a co-conspirator, she was stripped of her jewellery and cash, and driven out across the border.

Later, the king was brought to Bhaktapur and interned at the ancient palace there. A few years later, he was moved to the Hanumandhoka Royal Palace. Living under a protracted house arrest that lasted for as many as thirty-four years, and weathering many a storm, King Rajendra died in Kathmandu on 12 July 1881 at the age of sixty-eight. At the time of his death, his son, King Surendrabikram Shah, and his grandson, Crown Prince Trailokyabikram Shah, were not around to mourn for him; both had already passed away. His six-year-old son Prithvibirbikram Shah became the new crown prince.

The Kot Massacre perpetrated by Jungbahadur had considerably dented King Rajendra's political powers. Likewise, the Bhandarkhal Episode had rendered Queen Rajyalaxmi powerless. The Alou killings resulted in the exhaustion of all of Rajendra's powers, while Jungbahadur's were reinforced. Following this incident, no one surfaced on the political proscenium of Nepal who could possibly pose any challenge to the authority of Jungbahadur as long as he lived.

The massacre that took place at the Alou village in Parsa district is famous by the name of the Alou Episode in the annals of Nepal's history. Among those who died in the attack were Rambaksh Singh (King Rajendra's maternal uncle), Capt. Kirtibir Thapa, Lt Ambar Shahi, Lt Bhimbhakta Khawas, Subba Kalidas, Bodhman Karki, Jaharsingh Bhandari, Ramnath Upadhyaya, Kashinath, Badriban Khatri and Gayashankar Katuwal.

As many as eight attendants of Guruprasad Shah's were killed, along with thirty-five other members of the Shahi and Pande families, twenty Rajputs of Madhesh, eleven rebel soldiers of the Rajdal regiment, two Turkish riders, two of Nani Sahib's men and three ordinary citizens.

The number of people who were injured and fled across the border but reportedly died later remains unknown.

Altogether, twenty-three people sustained injuries in the attack, while six people, including priest Chandrakanta Aryal and civil servants Banabajir and Balabhadra Dhamala, were arrested and tied up in ropes.

There was no loss of lives on Jungbahadur's side, and only five of his soldiers sustained injuries.

Nine

The Death of Jungbahadur and the
Rana Repression of Revolt

Jungbahadur Kunwar apparently had the conspiratorial gene in him, perhaps inheriting it from the Thapas on his maternal side. In his first act of intrigue, he had killed his maternal uncle Mathbarsingh Thapa. Then he had exterminated all his adversaries by masterminding the Kot Massacre, in the process laying the foundation for the autocracy of the Ranas. The Bhandarkhal Episode came as an epilogue to the Kot Massacre, stripping Queen Rajyalaxmi of all her authority, finally leading to her banishment. Following the Alou incident, Jungbahadur could depose King Rajendra and enthrone Crown Prince Surendrabikram Shah, thereby catapulting himself to the position of the absolute ruler of Nepal.

Already, Jungbahadur had obtained from King Surendra the entire authority of governing the state by getting the latter's lalmohar affixed on the power-transfer document, on 20 September 1848. And, as if all this were not enough, he even made an attempt to ascend the throne—but he could not succeed. After winning the Nepal–Tibet war in 1855–56, he made a second bid to ascend the throne, but failed again. Yet, on 7 August 1856, he acquired for himself the title of Shree Teen Maharaja, thereby becoming the King of Kaski and Lamjung provinces; he was even presented a silver headgear by King Surendra, who had by now become subservient to Jungbahadur. Then, claiming that his predecessors were the descendants of the Ranas of Mewad, Jungbahadur also successfully acquired from the monarch the surname of Rana, thus transforming his entire family name from Kunwar-Kshettry to Kunwar-Rana, on 16 May 1848. Interestingly, it was only his family members who were entitled to the surname of Rana; the other Kunwars kept their original surname.

Jungbahadur then began meddling in the affairs of the state treasury. As he had recklessly taken out resources from the treasury, and even cut out the allowances to the royal palace, the king's residence started to bear a dark and abandoned look when compared to Jungbahadur's mansion at Thapathali. Shortly thereafter, he introduced the practice of issuing official orders and summons under his own name instead of the king's. This practice tended to undermine the significance and dignity of the institution of monarchy, while Jungbahadur's own position was considerably strengthened. All this while, as Jungbahadur was accumulating for himself all the power and authority, all his brothers were solidly behind him, thereby assisting him in laying the foundation for what essentially turned out to be a family regime.

The day Prime Minister Jungbahadur Kunwar Rana wore the silver headgear of the King of Kaski and Lamjung provinces, he also clearly outlined an order of succession.

According to this order, after him, his five brothers would take turns at holding the positions of the King of Kaski and Lamjung, and that of the prime minister; and after the brothers, his sons, namely Jagatjung and Jitjung Rana, would do the same.

Thus far, the going had been good. But soon after the publication of the roll that designated succession, Jungbahadur had a son, Padmajung, from his new wife. Some eight years later, he had a grandson, Yuddhapratapjung Rana, the son of Jagatjung. In the changed circumstances, Jungbahadur decided he needed to add his son Padmajung and the newborn grandson to the succession roll, along with two other sons from his mistress, in the order of seniority. And as Jungbahadur feared that the amended roll of succession which came into effect on 24 November 1867 would be violated, an affidavit was also issued as a preventive measure, which had the stamps of consent of Jungbahadur himself, his successors and King Surendra.

In fact, when the first roll of succession had been published, the Ranas had split into two distinct factions, sowing then and there the seeds of future conflicts between the two. Additions to the roll had further increased the prospects of such discords and quarrels. By the time the amendment came, Jungbahadur's two brothers, namely Bambahadur Rana and Gen. Krishnabahadur Rana, had died, while the third brother Badrinarsingh Rana had been consigned to exile as the Governor of Palpa. So, only three brothers, namely Runodeepsingh, Jagatshumsher and Dhirshumsher, were left as claimants to the succession list. After them came his three sons from legitimate wives, namely Jagatjung,

Jitjung and Padmajung, and two others from his mistress, namely Babarjung and Ranabirjung. Thereafter came the turn of grandson Yuddhapratapjung and then the cousins—Kedarnarsingh, Bambikram, Buddhibikram, Birshumsher, Ambarjung, etc.—in order of seniority in age.

Jungbahadur's cousin Kedarnarsingh Rana was behind grandson Yuddhapratapjung in the order of succession, although he was twenty-six years older than the latter. It was highly unlikely that Kedarnarsingh would be able to make it to the prime ministerial post. What was more, eleven other claimants, starting from Bambikram to Chandrashumsher, too, were older than Yuddhapratapjung; yet, they could not harbour any hope whatsoever about getting the post. Finding that their sons had thus fallen behind in the roll, Jagatshumsher and Dhirshumsher were disgruntled with their brother though they were not able to register any protest. They remained silent, waiting for their turn at the premiership so that they would be able to amend the roll in a manner suiting their convenience.

By this time, King Surendra's eldest son and heir apparent, Trailokya, had turned twenty. For Crown Prince Trailokya, the Ranas' tussle over the position of prime minister despite the Shah family's lawful rights to rule resembled the 'jackal's rule in the tiger's domain'. It was no small wonder then that he harboured the desire to replace Rana rule with one by his own Shah dynasty. But no one could even dare to look Jungbahadur squarely in the eye as long as he lived, let alone raise a voice against the Rana regime. And in Trailokya's particular case, Jungbahadur had given him the hands of three of his daughters in marriage, besides showering him with money and jewellery. What was more, Jungbahadur's sons, Jagatjung Rana and Jitjung Rana, had wed King Surendra's daughters, with Yuddhapratapjung being the son of one of them. The family ties were so close and interwoven that Trailokya would have had to ensure that the families of Jungbahadur Kunwar remained fully protected even in the unlikely event of the Rana rule coming to an end.

After he became prime minister, Jungbahadur had officially wed Hiranyagarbhakumari, a sister of Fattejung Shah's, who, in the final years of his life, had been in charge of the prime minister's household. Hiranyagarbhakumari had made up her mind that after her husband's death, the authority of the state should rest in the hands of Trailokya, who was also her son-in-law, rather than in the hands of Jungbahadur's brothers. As for Jungbahadur's son Jagatjung, he knew that once his uncles got hold of the reins of power, it would not be easy for him to lay hands on them. So a plan was quietly mapped out under which, following the death of Jungbahadur, Crown Prince Trailokya would seize the seat of power with the help of the regiments under Jungbahadur's command, while Jagatjung would become the prime minister.

At this point in time, the prominent Rana faction had three main characters: Runodeepsingh, Jagatshumsher and Dhirshumsher. Runodeepsingh was a religious scholar, while Jagatshumsher was a simpleton; however, both these brothers were supposedly addicted to marijuana and were not tough characters. Dhirshumsher, the youngest of the three, was the one with guts and valour—and he had no such addiction.

Dhirshumsher had got wind of Crown Prince Trailokya and Jagatjung's plan, and was staying vigilant.

However, on 26 January 1877, Jungbahadur, who had left for the Terai on a hunting expedition, suddenly died at Pattharghat of Rautahat, while his wife Hiranyagarbhakumari was alongside him. It was not possible for the grief-stricken queen to immediately send the news of her husband's demise to Crown Prince Trailokya in Kathmandu. However, General Amarjung Rana, by sending out runners at night, could convey the news to Runodeepsingh in Kathmandu within forty hours. The news reached Runodeepsingh and his brothers at a time when they believed that the crown prince as well as their cousin Jagatjung Rana posed some kind of a threat to them. So the sensitive message from the Terai was concealed all day and, as night fell, all the courtiers assembled and a team of all the Ranas who had been named in the roll of succession, led by Runodeepsingh, presented itself to King Surendrabikram Shah at the royal palace. The king was fast asleep in his room. He was woken up. Then, paying due respect to him by placing gold coins at his feet, Runodeepsingh and his brothers succeeded in obtaining from the king the stamp of approval on the document that vested them with the authority of Shree Teen Maharaja.

By hiding the news of Jungbahadur's death until they had got the king's approval for the order of succession, Runodeepsingh and his brothers had also successfully denied for the time being any contact between the crown prince and Jagatjung—this was indeed a big feat. Actually, Trailokya came to know of the changed context only after the bugle was played in salute to the new King of Kaski and Lamjung at Nasalchowk of the Hanumandhoka Royal Palace. Similarly, Jagatjung, who was at the Manohara Palace, over two miles from Kathmandu, also came to know of his father's death only after the nineteen-gun salute was fired in honour of the Shree Teen Maharaja. Thus, both Trailokya and Jagatjung were forced to remain inactive when the moment of truth came.

Amarjung Rana, who belonged to the Dhirshumsher camp, was in charge not only of the regiment that had accompanied Jungbahadur to Pattharghat but also its ammunition. Yet, Dhirshumsher was anxious about taking control over this regiment as soon as possible. Meanwhile, Hiranyagarbhakumari had asked for King Surendra's approval to become the Sati on the death of her husband. As it was vital to take the letter of approval from King Surendra to her, Dhirshumsher himself hurriedly departed for the Terai. But as Dhirshumsher feared that if the crown prince remained in the capital in the company of Jagatjung, there might be trouble, he literally forced Trailokya into a palanquin to be taken to Pattharghat.

The crown prince felt humiliated and insulted at Dhirshumsher's cunning conduct. Now his animosity against the Ranas grew intensely, and after returning from the Terai, he along with Jagatjung began weaving intrigues against the Rana rule. But overthrowing it was indeed a formidable task. Runodeepsingh had clamped a ban on courtiers meeting the crown prince, so Jagatjung was denied easy access to him. Under these circumstances, Trailokya was left with no choice but to make attempts at strengthening his own faction; to this effect, he started channelling messages through Tankanath

Upadhyaya and Homanath Upadhyaya, the sons of his maid at the palace.

By this time, another group, comprising the descendants of old-time courtiers, who felt inferior to the class to which the Ranas belonged, was active. During his time, Jungbahadur had recruited into the civil service the descendents of the nobles and courtiers who had either been killed, sent into exile or had had their property confiscated. These descendants thus harboured resentment against Jungbahadur and even sought revenge for the harsh acts against their forefathers. Much of their confiscated property had not been returned to them yet. Thus, this group, comprising ordinary courtiers, was waiting for an opportune moment to rise against the Rana regime.

Among the courtiers belonging to the disgruntled group was Colonel Shribikram Thapa, the son of General Mathbarsingh Thapa. The crown prince had won him over to his side. Also joining the Jagatjung camp was Colonel Indrasingh Tandon (brother of Sanaksingh), who was a member of the Courtiers' Council appointed by Jungbahadur. General Bambikram Rana also joined Jagatjung's faction, after receiving an assurance that he would get the office of commander-in-chief in the future dispensation.

As things stood, Crown Prince Trailokya wanted to act promptly. However, Jagatjung, who was known to indulge himself in the pleasures of life, was largely dejected and dispirited. 'How can I kill my uncles while I mourn the death of my father,' was how he viewed the situation.

Then, on 30 March 1878, barely two months after the death anniversary of Jungbahadur, Crown Prince Trailokya suddenly passed away, leaving behind a minor son. Now bereft of leadership, the faction in the crusade against the Ranas became rudderless. The elderly deduced that Crown Prince Trailokya had been murdered, and that Dhirshumsher was behind the plot—he had made the physicians administer poison to Trailokya. But as nobody dared to speak out against the Ranas, all were quiet over Trailokya's death.

When Trailokya had been clandestinely taking in members for his anti-Rana group, he had ensured that they were faithful, honest and trustworthy on all counts. It had been mandatory for a prospective member to take a vow of loyalty by touching the sacred tulsi plant as well as copper objects. Each member had to follow the strict directive that the group's activities be kept secret even from their wives and children; and they had been adhering to the directive strictly. Thus, Narendrabikram Shah, the brother of Trailokya, as well as Jagatjung's brothers, had been unaware of the anti-Rana movement. However, the foxy Dhirshumsher had got wind of it. So, posting spies at the places of the crown prince and Jagatjung, he had kept a close watch on the duo's activities. On their part, both Trailokya and Jagatjung knew quite well that Dhirshumsher had sent spies to their places; in fact, they knew who the spies were, and had remained wary of them.

In the summer of 1878, a spy named Ujir Giri, who was employed at the cowshed of Jagatjung, conveyed to Dhirshumsher that General Jagatjung Rana, while visiting the palace of Shree Teen Maharaja usually carried with him a pistol in the inside pocket of his jacket and that the pocket was always buttoned up for fear that the pistol would drop on the floor while he was paying obeisance to the prime minister. When Dhirshumsher took the matter to Prime Minister Runodeepsingh, naturally, the latter was startled. So when Jagatjung paid Runodeepsingh a visit that day, the prime minister decided to search his person before allowing him to enter. But no pistol was found on Jagatjung's body. Then, Runodeepsingh sent his trusted men to search the carriage that Jagatjung had mounted.

The carriage parked outside was found locked. Jagatjung was asked to hand over the key, but he showed reluctance to do so. Suspicion grew and they found the key in Jagatjung's pocket. Here it should be mentioned that Jagatjung, son of Jungbahadur who had earned fame by performing the rare feat of jumping into the Trisuli River on horseback from its tallest bridge, by now had become Nepal's hedonistic Wazid-Ali Shah. Jagatjung's large carriage, drawn by four horses, was equipped with a toilet attended by young maids who would unfasten and fasten his trousers when he went for urination. Jagatjung had been reluctant to hand over the key of the carriage for fear that his lavish lifestyle would be exposed. He wasn't a brave soul and nor was he carrying a pistol at this time.

When the doors of the carriage were opened, lo and behold, a young and pretty maid stood in attention by the toilet. But no pistol was found in the carriage. When the news was relayed to Runodeepsingh, he did not find it hard to convince himself that Jagatjung was innocent; he came to the conclusion that Dhirshumsher and his ilk were unnecessarily jealous of Jagatjung and that he posed no threat of any kind.

As for Dhirshumsher, he was not certain about what

exactly the anti-Rana group was up to. With the passing away of Trailokya, the group was near dissolution. It was during this time that Sangramsur Bista, one of the leading spirits behind the anti-Rana movement, was posted in the Terai by Runodeepsingh, and conferred with the title of Sirdar. At first, Sangramsur accepted the assignment and even expressed his gratefulness to the prime minister; however, being someone who had been employed at the armoury in Kathmandu, he felt he was unsuited for the jungles and farm fields of the Terai where malaria lurked. So he quit his job and went on to live in retirement in the capital.

After lying dormant for about a year, the anti-Rana group revived itself in a new form and under a new leadership, following the death of Commander-in-Chief Jagatshumsher in April 1879. Following Crown Prince Trailokya's death, his brother Narendrabikram Shah had set his eyes on the title of crown prince. But the Ranas had denied him this stature by anointing Trailokya's infant son Prithvibirbikram Shah as the crown prince. Although what the Ranas had done was in complete conformity with norms and tradition, Prince Narendrabikram Shah had taken it otherwise—he felt he had been treated unjustly. Thereafter, Narendrabikram began to resent the Ranas, ultimately leading him to assume the leadership of the reactivated anti-Rana group.

Prime Minister Runodeepsingh Rana and Commander-in-Chief Dhirshumsher were the key players in the Rana-led administration. Prince Narendrabikram entertained the notion that if these two Rana brothers could be crushed, their descendants and other Ranas would automatically flee and then power would flow into his hands smoothly. In pursuance of this plan, Narendrabikram met Shribikramsingh Thapa, who had been a member of the anti-Rana faction built up by Trailokya earlier. Shribikram brought in Sangramsur Bista to rejoin the group and, on the urging of the duo (Shribikram and Sangramsur), Narendrabikram became ready to assume the leadership of the anti-Rana clique. Now a debate ensued over whether or not to protect the interests of the sons and grandsons of Jungbahadur's, who were close relations of Narendrabikram Shah, in the event of the end of the Rana rule. Finally, it was agreed that the lives of these sons and grandsons of Jungbahadur's would be protected, but that they wouldn't be given any space in the future council of ministers, and nor would they be assigned the position of general in any regiment.

The anti-Rana group's plan was to stage a coup by murdering both Prime Minister Runodeepsingh Rana and Commander-in-Chief Dhirshumsher Rana simultaneously, thereby paving the way for the ascension of Narendrabikram to the throne. It was decided that once the Ranas were overthrown, only senior nobles and courtiers, barring, of course, those belonging to the Rana family, would be taken into the council of ministers or appointed as generals. Possibly, it was also agreed that Shribikramsingh Thapa would become the prime minister, while Sangramsur Bista would assume the position of the commander-in-chief. And putting forth the example of the Kot Massacre, which had been the handiwork of some twenty people acting on behalf of Jungbahadur, it was decided that only twenty people out of the descendents of the senior courtiers would form the core group of the anti-Rana movement. Meanwhile, Shivaprasad Aryal and Bhairabbahadur Khatri, who were staying home after having been dismissed from service, also joined the group.

Notwithstanding all this, the group remained inactive for some time. Jungbahadur had given Narendrabikram Shah not only his daughter, but also loads of cash and jewellery as dowry and gifts. So, with plentiful resources at his disposal, the prince was in the habit of showering rewards and baksheesh on his followers like Shribikramsingh Thapa. He was also biding his time, both chalking out and discarding action plans. The group achieved nothing for nearly two years.

Meanwhile, a strange incident occurred. Shribikramsingh, Sangramsur and other members of the anti-Rana group had taken the oath of secrecy of 'not revealing the objective of the group' even to their wives, sons and brothers, and in the event of any one of them being arrested perchance, he would be prepared to die, but would under no circumstances implicate other members. But one day, Sangramsur happened to tell his wife in a fit of anger: 'You will either become the queen or a widow. Shut up!' Colonel Laldhoj Bista, a neighbour, reportedly overheard Sangramsur, and he promptly passed this on to his relative, Dhirshumsher. Dhirshumsher was always wary of adversaries. As he had grabbed power by intrigue, he was constantly tormented by the fear that he too would fall victim to an intrigue some day. He surmised that Sangramsur was definitely involved in a plot against him.

Then, taking Laldhoj along with him, Dhirshumsher rushed to Prime Minister Runodeepsingh Rana and submitted: 'Your Highness! I guess some conspiracy is afoot against us.

We will come to know about the conspiracy if Sangramsur Bista is arrested and flogged; thus, we can save ourselves; otherwise, the lives of all Ranas are in peril.' But the simple-minded Runodeepsingh could not immediately believe that a conspiracy was-being hatched against him. 'Why would anyone conspire against me when I have done no harm to anybody?' the prime minister snapped back. And about Sangramsur, he said, 'He is a hashish addict, so he may say anything; we should not worry over such things.' Thus, Sangramsur was spared punishment. Actually, Runoudeepsingh Rana himself was a hashish addict. But he believed that nobody outside his household knew that he smoked hashish regularly.

On 17 May 1881, King Surendrabikram Shah died, and his grandson and Crown Prince Prithvibirbikram Shah, a minor, ascended the throne. Less than two months later, on 12 July 1881, King Rajendra, the deposed monarch who had long been held under house arrest, also passed away. So, with a five-year-old boy as the king and a philosopher as the prime minister, Commander-in-Chief Dhirshumsher had now become Nepal's undeclared but undisputed, absolute ruler. Yet he feared and remained highly suspicious of the group led by Prince Narendrabikram. He began to work on a plan to drive Narendrabikram away from the capital to Gorkha, under some pretext. But this he could not do without the approval of Prime Minister Runodeepsingh. Interestingly, when the subject was broached, the prime minister expressed the view that only after the one-year period of mourning of King Rajendrabikram's death could the prince be permitted to leave the capital. Dhirshumsher muttered under his breath, yet he was obliged to stay quiet. In the meantime, Narendrabikram had learnt from the grapevine that Dhirshumsher was working overtime to send him into exile. Shribikramsingh Thapa and his followers were outraged at the news and they began to clandestinely chalk out a new plot against the Ranas.

Jungbahadur had erected a grand temple in the forest of Mrigasthali in Pashupati; inside it was a magnificent statue of Biswaroopa Bhagawati. Every year, the temple witnessed a grand and elaborate worship ceremony of the goddess. During such occasions, gambling, otherwise prohibited, was allowed on the temple grounds for thirty-six hours. For a long time, every year, members of the Rana families used to assemble at the temple precincts on that day of entertainment and recreation, feasting and gambling. In the year 1881, this ritual of worship was held in mid-October. That was when Narendrabikram and his cronies planned to pull off the murder of both the prime minister and the commander-in-chief, while the duo would be engaged in gambling at the temple. As per the plan, on the previous day, explosives had been placed at vantage points, while the would-be killers had taken up their respective positions.

As anticipated by the plotters, Runodeepsingh and Dhirshumsher were indeed gambling at the temple that day. But by a strange coincidence, some four to five Brahmin priests, including Dwijaraj Pande and Lokraj Pande, unexpectedly happened to be in the company of the prime minister and his brother. If the explosives were detonated as planned, the objective—of killing both the prime minister and the commander-in-chief—would have been met. But then, the Brahmins too would have died, which would have been blasphemous as tradition forbade the killing of a Brahmin. Thus, the entire plot was aborted.

About a month and a half later, on 1 December 1881, the coronation of Prithvibirbikram Shah was to be solemnized in a grand manner. The intervening period was spent in making preparations for the official crowning of Prithvibirbikram. According to the schedule, some ten days after the coronation, Prime Minister Runodeepsingh Rana was to leave the capital for the Terai on a hunting expedition, and two or three days before leaving, he was to pay homage at the temples of Pashupati and Guheswori. On the same day that Runodeepsingh was to visit Pashupati, Dhirshumsher, too, was scheduled to visit the firing range at the eastern end of the Pashupati forest. As per the itinerary, Dhirshumsher was to travel in a carriage via the road leading to the Manohara Palace, while he would return on horseback through the jungle to meet Runodeepsingh at the temple. The anti-Rana group headed by Narendrabikram, having known about the programme in advance, now hurriedly chalked out a plot to make a bid on the lives of the prime minister and the commander-in-chief.

All along, Narendrabikram Shah and his followers had remained truly scared of Dhirshumsher's powers. They didn't dare confront him face to face. So, the plot was to ambush Dhirshumsher while he returned from the firing range by detonating explosives at the 'Slippery Slope' at the southern end of the Pashupati forest. Then, as soon as the news of Dhirshumsher's murder was received, Prime Minister Runodeepsingh, too, would be murdered while he would be walking the distance between the Pashupati temple and the Guheswori shrine. Accordingly, the would-be murderers had taken up their positions. But incidentally, that day, Dhirshumsher's carriage broke down on the way to the firing range, forcing him to return to his mansion cancelling the day's programmes. Thus, the plan could not be carried out, while Runodeepsingh, too, returned home without any trouble on the way. Then, as per schedule, after a couple of days, Runodeepsingh left for the Terai on his hunting expedition. Thus, the second plot, too, had failed.

Prince Narendrabikram was truly saddened by the failures of the attempts to take the lives of the prime minister and the commander-in-chief. And as he now anticipated that he would soon be forced into exile, he promptly started devoting his time to chalking out a third plot.

During this time, Lt Uttardhoj Bhandari, a grandson of Gen. Gagansingh Bhandari, served as an officer in charge of the security guards at Dhirshumsher's mansion. With his help, anybody could easily make his way at night to the chamber where Dhirshumsher slept, and could also safely return after 'accomplishing the job'. So, Narendrabikram had planned to take Uttardhoj into his group. Thus, with the help of a third person who had also taken the oath of secrecy, Narendrabikram met Uttardhoj at the premises of a famous temple. After putting a necklace of precious pearls as a gift around Uttardhoj's neck, the prince told him, 'After the plan is successfully implemented, you will become a general, but for now, accept the title of colonel.' However, Uttardhoj was an immature man given to fits of frivolity. He could not keep the news of this encounter with the prince to himself, and leaked out the matter to his elder sister who happened to be the wife of Gen. Badrinarsingh Rana.

The essence of Narendrabikram's third plot lay in doing away with Dhirshumsher at the latter's mansion on the night of 11 January 1882. The prince believed that once Dhirshumsher was murdered, all the Ranas, including Prime Minister Runodeepsingh, who was on a hunting mission to the Terai, would flee. He had also dispatched a few of his trusted men to the Terai to exterminate Runodeepsingh should the latter decline to flee. Meanwhile, startled by the news of the plot as reeled out to her by her brother, Badrinarsingh's wife first scolded Uttardhoj and then produced him before Dhirshumsher to make him spill out the entire details.

For his part, Dhirshumsher, exercising tremendous patience, extracted from Uttardhoj one by one the names, surnames and addresses of the conspirators. Dhirshumsher's plan was to seize all his foes all at once before they became aware of what was happening. As Gen. Bambikram Rana was one of his trusted cousins, Dhirshumsher considered asking for his help in seizing the conspirators. Dhirshumsher knew that as some of the conspirators had already made it to the camp of the prime minister in the Terai, any delay in arresting them would be fraught with danger. Thus, he planned to arrest them all on the night of 6 January 1882. Then he promptly sent out a letter to his brother Runodeepsingh in the Terai asking for the arrest the same night of the would-be murderers who had made it to the hunting camp. The letter reached there by the evening of 6 January. Thus, that very night, the conspiring officers, including Gen. Ambarjung Kunwar Rana, Col. Amarbikram Thapa and Sirdar Shivaprasad Aryal, were arrested from their tents. And the next day, all the arrested men were dispatched to Kathmandu in chains.

On the same day, Dhirshumsher also sent the soldiers of the Kalibox regiment, which was under his command, to encircle the residences of the rebels, including that of Shribikram Thapa, who were then arrested and brought to the commander-in-chief's mansion, to be held in detention separately. However, Sirdar Sangramsur Bista, Captain Bhairabbahadur, Captain Shumsherjung Pande and his son Singhjung Pande managed to escape from their houses. In fact, Dhirshumsher himself helped in the escape of Major Deepbahadur Shah, a brother-in-law of the commander-in-chief's son. On the third day of this crackdown, Singhjung Pande was found lying dead on the bank of the Dhobikhola River—he had been poisoned. On this day, Sangramsur Bista, who had hid himself in a flour mill, was also arrested. Dhirshumsher was furious with Sangramsur, so he and Bambikram Rana flogged him mercilessly.

Meanwhile, a new twist took place in the whole episode. Sangramsur Bista, who was being flogged, submitted to Dhirshumsher that a conspiracy had been hatched against the Ranas even earlier under the leadership of Crown Prince Trailokya and that Bambikram Rana too had been involved in it. At this, Bambikram's face turned pale, and his mouth dried up. Dhirshumsher was now convinced that Bambikram too was a party to the anti-Rana conspiracy, and he gave orders to flog Bambikram. With the flogging of Bambikram all the secrets behind the plots that had been futilely hatched from time to time under the leadership of Trailokya were revealed. Following these revelations, Col. Indrasingh Tandon and Col. Amritsingh Adhikari, who were on official tours to Dhulikhel and Nuwakot respectively, were arrested and produced at Dhirshumsher's mansion in a few days. All these 'criminals' were held separately. Then, in order to extract more information, Dhirshumsher ordered the flogging of them all. But Indrasingh Tandon and Shivaprasad Aryal were spared from being beaten black and blue on account of their advanced age and also because both had broken their legs while attempting to flee.

Thus, by resorting to flogging and other methods of intimidation, Dhirshumsher succeeded in finding out that he and his family members had been the targets of umpteen plots and intrigues in the past. He also used the opportunity to settle scores with all his foes, including those whom he suspected of harbouring ill will against him. It is said that even Indrasingh Tandon, who was spared the flogging, was so terrified that he was prepared to confess to any charges that would be brought against him.

By the time Runodeepsingh Rana returned from his hunting expedition, the commander-in-chief had already obtained the red-seal approval from the six-year-old king Prithvibirbikram Shah, thus setting things ready for the execution of the twenty-two schemers. Runodeepsingh hurried up from the Terai and entered his mansion at Narayanhity on the midnight of 15 January 1882. The twenty-two culprits who were in the commander-in-chief's execution roll were carried in a *kharpan* (a goods carrier suspended from the shoulders) to be produced at the prime minister's residence at daybreak; they were in chains and handcuffs. Of course, Dhirshumsher was overseeing the entire operation.

Although advanced in years, Runodeepsingh used to carry the infant king on his back whenever Prithvibirbikram Shah needed to move around; and the prime minister pretended to relish this job. So the morning after he came back from the Terai, Runodeepsingh—perched on the shoulders of his orderly who was holding an umbrella—and carrying the minor king on his back, appeared at his palace courtyard to take a look at the conspirators.

Among them were Shribikram Thapa and Indrasingh Tandon. Until then, the Ranas had believed that Indrasingh Tandon was one of their well-wishers. Pointing to Shribikram, the prime minister asked the one-eyed Indrasingh, 'He must have thought of taking revenge because we killed his grandfather Mathbarsingh Thapa; that can be understood, but you we had held in high respect in the position of a courtier; why did you turn a traitor?' In response, Indrasingh, who had by now become a fierce opponent of the Ranas, recounted one by one all the vices of the Rana rule. Runodeepsingh was taken aback by Indrasingh's remarks, but refused to make any comment; he then turned towards Dhirshumsher and asked him to hand Indrasingh over to the executioner. Thus, giving orders to put the courtier to death, Runodeepsingh returned to his room.

Some twenty members of the 'Sangramsur conspirators' band' were less than thirty-six years old. They were mostly young adults with plenty of vigour and courage. All clearly saw that disaster was imminent for them, yet they felt that they had nothing more to fear now. So, rather unexpectedly, they started raising slogans: 'Long Live the King!' 'Death to the Rana Family!' Dhirshumsher, his eyes burning with fury, however could only listen mutely. That very day, that is, on 16 January 1882, the twenty plotters were split into six different groups and beheaded one by one. The following were the anti-Rana insurgents who were put to death on that day:

The Thapas: Col. Shribikramsingh Thapa, Col. Amarbikramsingh Thapa, Maj. Sansarbikramsingh Thapa, Capt. Samarbikramsingh Thapa, Capt. Sumsherjung Thapa and . . . Singh Thapa (first part of the first name unknown).

The Bistas: Sirdar Sangramsur Bista, Capt. Narabahadur Bista, Capt. Bhojraj Bista, Lt Suryapratap Bista, Lt Keshar Bista and one of his brothers.

Others: Col. Indrasingh Tandon, Ranadal Karki, Subedar Pahalman Karki, Banka Adhikari, Capt. Faudasingh Gurung, Yogbikram Pande, Capt. Bakhtabar Shahi and Lt Chattradhoj Shahi.

The same day, Col. Amritsingh Adhikari and Lt Chhetrabahadur Bista, the twenty-year-old brother of Sangramsu Bista's, had also been taken out for execution, but were later recalled, supposedly for renewed examination and to extort confessions.

The property in the valley held by all the conspirators was

confiscated, while all of their family members were shunted out of the valley.

Among the conspirators, there were also five Brahmins—Shivaprasad Aryal, Digvijaya Upadhyaya, Homanath, Tankanath and priest Kana Bhatta; but as tradition prohibited their execution, they were given life sentences. However, before sending them out to serve their terms in Palpa, they were paraded in the three cities of the Kathmandu valley with their heads tonsured and a piglet slung on each of their shoulders, to the accompaniment of music, for three consecutive days, starting from 1 February. Four days later, Amritsingh, who had been recalled from execution, was eventually put to death, as he revealed nothing fresh; also executed were the recently arrested Col. Birmansingh Basnet and Lokbahadur Thapa, while Lt. Bhubansingh Khatri's lips were torched with hot iron. And, some five to six other people, including Chhetrabahadur Bista, Indranath Upadhyaya and Saligram, were given prison terms of six years each. Further, three people, including Indradhoj Lohani, were sent back to their houses in the hills and detained there. Then a search was mounted for three persons, including Deepbahadur Shah and Bhairabbahadur Khatri, who were absconding.

After the execution, on 16 February, a meeting of the Courtiers' Council was convened in which a kind of drama was enacted to show that justice had been delivered. The infant king Prithvibirbikram, his mother and stepmother attended the meeting, which was essentially a forum that sought to legalize Dhirshumsher's brutal act of crushing his adversaries. Following a debate on the issue, the council also established that both Prince Narendrabikram Shah and Bambikram Rana were culprits, and then both were sent to the Chunargadh Fort in Allahabad, India, where they joined the princesses from Afghanistan who were also imprisoned there. While Bambikram's property was not confiscated, the cash and jewellery worth 1.8 million rupees found during the search of Narendrabikram Shah's house, was impounded. The royal palace was compelled to watch all this helplessly.

Dhirshumsher was also able to keep Padmajung Rana, one of Jungbahadur's sons, in detention for a few days, on the ground of suspicion or by getting others to implicate him as a conspirator. But at the council meeting, Queen Mother Lalitrajyeswori and Runodeepsingh's wife Haripriya Devi pleaded innocence on his behalf, and he was cleared of the charges, and after about four months reinstated to his position of commander-general of the south.

While all this was taking place, Jungbahadur's eldest son, Gen. Jagatjung Rana, was on a pilgrimage to India. He chose to remain in exile there, fearing suppression from his uncle Dhirshumsher who had by now firmly established his power in the country. On a special request of the Nepalese kingdom, the British once kept Jagatjung under house arrest in Calcutta.

The faction formed to rise in revolt against the rule of the Ranas had been quite formidable. And the revolt could possibly have succeeded but for the act of betrayal by the frivolous Uttardhoj Bhandari. It was the unfortunate leaking of the faction's secret that had resulted in both the ruthless suppression of the conspirators and the subsequent reign of terror over the Nepalese people. For at least fifty years thereafter, no Nepalese would dare speak out against the Rana rule that continued unobstructed for a long period of time.

All these events took place in the month of Magh of the year 1938 Bikram Sambat, corresponding to January/ February 1882 of the Gregorian calendar. Thus, in the records of Nepal's history, these events are collectively known as the Thirty-Eight-Year Episode.

Published in 1956 under the title 'The Rana Rule and Conspiracy' in the Nepalese-language monthly journal *Sharada*

Ten

The Brutal Murder of Runodeepsingh Rana

(1)

Jungbahadur Kunwar Rana had sown the seeds of division and conflict among the Rana families by establishing the order of succession to the offices of Shree Teen Maharaja and the prime minister. In the order that provided for seniority according to age, he had, however, placed his grandsons before his brothers, and this perhaps was the leading cause behind the intra-family feuding. As a consequence, the Rana families were split into two power groups: one comprising the sons and grandsons of Jungbahadur, and the other of Dhirshumsher and his sons. Thus, one group came to be known as the Jung faction and the other as the Shumsher faction.

Generally speaking, nobody had dared to differ with Jungbahadur, but his brothers and cousins had expressed their discontent with the roll of succession right from the beginning. Dhirshumsher, for one, had resolved even before the death of Jungbahadur that once he grabbed the office of the prime minister, he would reshuffle the names on the roll so as to make his sons the immediate successors. It is often said that Dhirshumsher used to tell his sons, 'Whoever has the sword has the palace,' meaning, only the one who could display the might and valour of the sword would be able to enjoy kingly comforts and pleasures.

During the first phase of Prime Minister Runodeepsingh Rana's administration, a politically potent anti-Rana group had been active in plots and machinations. But thanks to the extraordinary vigilance shown by Dhirshumsher, the group had been eliminated before it could successfully execute any of its schemes, and its members had been crushed, rather brutally. In the process, twenty-three persons, including Col. Shribikramsingh Thapa, had been beheaded, while twelve men had been imprisoned, and seven others forced into exile. Following this act of suppression, Dhirshumsher became the de facto ruler of Nepal, with Prime Minister Runodeepsingh rendered to a state wherein he could ignore Dhirshumsher's advice only at his own peril. Thus began the joint rule of the two brothers—one the prime minister and the other the commander-in-chief.

Alerted by the Thirty-Eight-Year Episode, the two brothers had moved the infant king Prithvibirbikram from his traditional residence of the Hanumandhoka Palace to Runodeepsingh's private mansion at Narayanhity. All three of the king's mothers were the daughters of Jungbahadur Rana. While it might have been essential for the second queen mother, the king's own mother, to accompany her son to the Narayanhity mansion, the senior queen mother, who was the patron of the monarch and therefore the regent (as per the prevalent practice in the Nepalese royal family, both offices were reserved for the seniormost queen mother), too, was called over to Narayanhity along with her daughter, her only offspring. The third queen mother, who had no offspring, was left to stay back at the Hanumandhoka Palace. It was but natural that the first and second queen mothers were jealous of each other as is likely between two stepsisters, but the senior queen mother was supposedly more attached to her stepson Prithvibirbikram Shah than to her own daughter. Yet, the Ranas of the Shumsher faction worked overtime to quietly spread the rumour that the senior queen mother wished that her daughter ascend the throne rather than her stepson.

For Gen. Jagatjung Rana, Jangbahadur's eldest son, the news of the murders and crushing of the anti-Rana plot were frightening enough to dissuade him from returning home after his pilgrimage in India. Earlier, he too had been involved when Crown Prince Trailokya had conspired against the Ranas. So he was tormented by the fact that, given the opportunity, Dhirshumsher would surely attempt to settle old scores. Meanwhile, because he had failed to return home in time, the prime minister and the commander-in-chief had struck Jagatjung's name off from the roll of succession, replacing him by his younger brother, Gen. Jitjung Rana. Padmajung Rana, Jungbahadur's youngest son, too, had been dismissed from his office, suspected of a role in the anti-Rana conspiracy, and replaced by Ranabirjung. So, all the Ranas named in the roll after Padmajung had automatically climbed two steps in the ladder of succession.

One day in March 1883, the stores of Nepalese businessmen in Lhasa were suddenly vandalized and looted. Despite correspondence spanning a year's period, the administrators in Tibet refused to compensate them for their losses, and so Nepal started preparing for an invasion. Gen. Padmajung was then called in for service and appointed as the commander of the troops that would march via Kerung. Now his former position was restored in the roll of succession. However, the invasion was averted after Tibet vowed to give compensation. All these events took place in June 1884.

On 14 October 1884, Dhirshumsher Rana suddenly met his death—he was eating bird meat when a bone got stuck in his throat. Following Dhirshumsher's demise, Jitjung Rana succeeded him as the commander-in-chief, while all the other brothers and nephews climbed up one step in the roll of succession. As of 22 November 1884, the roll of succession to the office of the prime minister ran as follows:

1. Prime Minister Runodeepsingh Rana, 59 (fifth brother of Jungbahadur)
2. Commander-in-Chief Jitjung Rana, 36 (son of Jungbahadur)
3. Commander General Padmajung Rana, 28 (son of Jungbahadur)
4. Commander General Ranabirjung Rana, 34 (son of Jungbahadur)
5. Commander General Yuddhapratapjung Rana, 19 (son of Jagatjung)

6.   Commander General Kedarnarsingh Rana, 46 (son of Badrinarsingh)

7.   General Birshumsher Rana, 33 (son of Dhirshumsher)

8.   General Amarjung Rana, 30 (son of Jagatshumsher)

9.   General Dhojnarsingh Rana, 25 (son of Badrinarsingh)

10. General Khadgashumsher Rana, 24 (son of Dhirshumsher)

11. General Bhupendrashumsher Rana, 24 (son of Jagatshumsher)

12. General Ranashumsher Rana, 24 (son of Dhirshumsher)

13. General Devshumsher Rana, 23 (son of Dhirshumsher)

14. Colonel Chandrashumsher Rana, 22 (son of Dhirshumsher)

15. Colonel Bhimshumsher Rana, 20 (son of Dhirshumsher)

16. Colonel Fatteshumsher Rana, 19 (son of Dhirshumsher)

17. Colonel Lalitshumsher Rana, 17 (son of Dhirshumsher)

18. Colonel Jeetshumsher Rana, 16 (son of Dhirshumsher)

19. Colonel Juddhashumsher Rana, 10, (son of Dhirshumsher)

Though Dhirshumsher was said to be unfavourably disposed towards his nephews Jagatjung Rana and Jitjung Rana, he had looked up to his issueless elder brother Runodeepsingh as a father figure. Right from the beginning, he had helped his brother discharge official responsibilities. So after Dhirshumsher's death, Runodeepsingh became helpless and vulnerable in some ways. While Runodeepsingh tried to maintain strict neutrality in the tussle between the two different Rana factions, he had resolved to make Jagatjung, Jungbahadur's eldest son, his successor, as he was mindful of the contributions Jungbahadur had made in ushering in the Rana rule. All along, Runodeepsingh had believed in Jagatjung's innocence; he was of the opinion that Jagatjung had been stripped of his position because of Dhirshumsher's prejudice and that the former would certainly have succeeded Dhirshumsher as the prime minister had he not been driven out of office. Runodeepsingh's wife Haripriya, too, endorsed these views. She was hand in glove with the senior queen mother, Jagatjung's sister, and both were working out schemes in order to prove Jagatjung's innocence and to secure him his rightful place as the successor to Runodeepsingh.

In the process, the duo reminded Runodeepsingh that Crown Prince Trailokyabikram Shah and Gen. Jagatjung Rana had not done anything wrong, and that they had been falsely implicated in the conspiracy after Dhirshumsher extracted confessions from Bambikram Rana and others by having them beaten up; they also told him that Col. Indrasingh Tandon, who had been beheaded, had been innocent. The simple-minded man that Runodeepsingh was, he adjudged the duo's views as right, and therefore decided to recall Jagatjung from India. But as there was the possibility of other brothers and nephews rising in revolt if Jagatjung was called back and his place in the roll of succession restored right away, he was put in chains and held under house arrest after he entered Nepalese territory. And before Jagatjung was brought to the capital, he was told that his detention would last till he was cleared by the justice system.

Fissures now grew in the relationship between Jagatjung and his brother Jitjung Rana as the latter could see that with the return of Jagatjung, he would lose his turn to be the prime minister. Indeed, when preparations had been under way to call Jagatjung back, Jitjung had left for Calcutta, with property in tow, saying that he needed to 'seek treatment for his eyes' there. Thus, the office of the commander-in-chief was temporarily handed over to his younger brother Padmajung Rana.

Runodeepsingh wanted to clear Jagatjung of what he believed to be 'fictitious' charges. With this end in view, Prince Narendrabikram Shah and Bambikram Rana, too, were called back to the capital from the fort of Chunargadh so that the charges against them could be re-examined. Runodeepsingh's view was that if they were questioned mildly, they would deny their participation in the anti-Rana revolt, and on that very basis, he would be able to clear them of all the charges. While being questioned, Narendrabikram said, 'The charge of conspiracy is completely false. I have committed no crime. I am innocent.' But in the case of Bambikram Rana, he was flogged while being questioned, and he confessed that he was involved in hatching a conspiracy. So, as a punishment, he was shunted out to Dhankuta. After Bambikram's confession, Runodeepsingh found it hard to fully absolve Jagatjung of the charges against him. So, he was kept under house arrest in his grand Manohara mansion. The prime minister was still sympathetic towards Jagatjung, and he would occasionally call him to his residence for consultations. There, Jagatjung could also quite often meet the senior queen, his sister, who would dole out assurances of his release from house arrest.

A few days later began what could be described as the second bid to prove Jagatjung's innocence. The senior queen, in her capacity as the regent, prepared a dharmapatra aimed at not only putting Jagatjung in the clear, but also establishing him as Runodeepsingh's successor. In a nutshell, the document read: 'We will accept if the succession goes from Runodeepsingh to Jagatjung Rana. We will have no objection to this.' But, for Padmajung Rana, the acting commander-in-chief and thus the next claimant to the office of the prime minister, this trust document came like a bolt out of the blue. However, he did not oppose it; he signed it, albeit unwillingly, knowing full well that the prime minister, after all, wanted to restore the place of his brother ahead of him in the roll of succession. The others who were placed below Padmajung in the succession order too gave their consent. But Dhirshumsher's eldest son, Birshumsher, and his brothers fiercely opposed the trust paper. While Runodeepsingh chose to stay silent about this opposition, the senior queen mother, the regent, was embittered by it. One day, in a fit of anger, she, on some excuse, got the Ranas of the Shumsher family, including Birshumsher, locked up in the garage of the premier's mansion for as long as ten hours.

The second queen mother, Prithvibirbikram's mother, opposed Jagatjung's reinstatement. And it was she who forced Gen. Padmajung Rana to vouch for the release of Birshumsher and his brothers from the garage lock-up. After the lock-up episode, Birshumsher and his brothers could see that their future was not all that secure and that they had to think of ways to keep themselves safe.

The Shumsher family clearly also knew that if they remained quiet and inactive, Jagatjung would grab power on the death of Runodeepsingh, and then they would all be driven away to the Terai or the hills. The overambitious Shumsher brothers were not the kind of personalities who could remain content merely with making ends meet; indeed, they were greatly envious of the riches as well as the honour acquired by Jungbahadur's sons and grandsons. While their father Dhirshumsher had passed on to them the dictum that 'whoever has the sword has the palace', they adopted as their motto the saying that 'either you rule over Hastinapur* or dwell under the turf'.

They nurtured the desire to build big castles and palaces, and stack up their ill-gotten wealth in foreign banks—all by the power of the sword. But they knew that sidelining Jagatjung would be no easy task—Runodeepsingh favoured him greatly, as did the senior queen mother, the regent. Thus, as they did not have the patience to wait till the natural death of the prime minister in order to mark the beginning of the rule of the Shumsher-Ranas, they resolved to overthrow the Jung-Rana regime, even if it meant putting their uncle Runodeepsingh to death.

In those days, the festival of Indrajatra used to be celebrated with great fanfare in the capital, Kathmandu. It was the custom that, to mark the occasion, the king, other members of the royal family and the prime minister used to stay at the Hanumandhoka Royal Palace for about ten days. Birshumsher and his brothers decided that this was the occasion to kill the prime minister. According to the plan, the murder would then be blamed on Ranabirjung Rana, and based on this charge, they would go about decimating not only Ranabirjung but also other members of the Jung-Rana family. The plan was to culminate

---

* A mythical kingdom

with the seizure of the minor monarch from whom the three-moon headband of the Maharaja would be obtained. As active support of the royal family was deemed essential to realize this plan, the second queen mother was taken into confidence by promising her a special annual grant of Rs 300,000.

However, the plan had to be aborted after Ranabirjung Rana got wind of it, and he went over to the royal palace to alert Col. Gambhir Katuwal, a bodyguard to the prime minister. Later, when Padmajung informed Runodeepsingh of the conspiracy, the latter simply laughed it away as something that couldn't be believed.

All this while, Runodeepsingh was waiting for that opportune moment when he could make Jagatjung his successor. Around this time, rumours were rife that a Russian attack on India was imminent. Thus, the British, as a means of assuring the Indians of their supremacy, planned a huge military exercise in Delhi. And on the request of the Indian government, Nepal decided to send 2000 of its own soldiers to participate in the military exercise in India. Runodeepsingh's plan was to send Gen. Birshumsher Rana and his brothers with the Nepalese contingent leaving for India, and as soon as the contingent crossed the Ganges River, to appoint Jagatjung as his successor, before he himself left for India on a pilgrimage. On their part, knowing that Gen. Birshumsher would be given the command of the contingent bound for India, the general and his brothers started making their own plans—to replace the Jung-Rana rule with one of their own; they knew that the 2000-strong contingent leaving for India would come in handy for this undertaking.

When the soldiers and officers of this contingent were named, the officers were mostly the Shumsher brothers. On the face of it, for a few days these officers seemed to concentrate their efforts on providing training to the members of the India-bound contingent. Actually, the Shumsher brothers were trying to use the contingent to grab power by doing away with Maharaja Runodeepsingh. Towards this end, Col. Kesharsingh Thapa, a maternal uncle of Khadgashumsher, was won over, and through him, Laxmibhakta Poudel, an adviser to the prime minister, and Gambhir Katuwal, a security officer, were also roped in. In fact, initially, Laxmibhakta and Gambhir had not wanted to help in the plot to kill Runodeepsingh; they agreed to help the Shumsher brothers only after they were told that Runodeepsingh would be arrested and sent on a pilgrimage to Kashi. The duo had also been enticed with the carrot of economic gains—each of them had been promised Rs 50,000.

At this time, Birshumsher and his brothers felt that the only threat they faced was from Ranabirjung Rana. It became essential to know whether Ranabirjung had got wind of their plot. In the meantime, the festival of Tihar arrived. It was customary that, to mark the festival, gambling, otherwise banned, was allowed for five days. The grand residence of Padmajung Rana at Thapathali was the hub of the gambling activities. Ranabirjung Rana was a frequent visitor to the place. During the festivities, Birshumsher and his brothers went over to Padmajung's palace, and enjoyed gambling for a couple of days, mingling with one and all. Among those gathered there for fun and enjoyment were many nobles, courtiers and military officers. In their exchanges with these people, the Shumsher brothers were able to read their minds. Now convinced that nobody suspected them of foul play, the Shumsher brothers decided to go ahead with the execution of their plot.

Runodeepsingh had told Birshumsher and his brothers that once they left for India for the military exercise, he himself would be going to the Terai on a hunting expedition. In fact, soon after the festival of Dasain that preceded Tihar, he had sent out in advance a party of soldiers and officials to make arrangements for the hunting trip. Then, on 10 November 1885, the day after the Tihar festival, the Rifel Regiment accompanying the prime minister's team left Kathmandu, and halted at Balaju. But Runodeepsingh was still held up in Kathmandu, as Birshumsher and his associates had not left for Delhi yet.

Actually, instead of looking for the right time to depart for Delhi, the Shumsher brothers were waiting for that opportune moment when they could put their uncle Runodeepsingh to death. They found out that a Sunday, 22 November 1885— the eighth day of the waxing moon—was considered to be inauspicious for the prime minister, and planned to end his life that night. A message was delivered to the prime minister, saying that the military contingent was all set to depart for India at dawn on 23 November.

However, in the meantime, an ill omen in the form of a vulture alighted on the roof of Runodeepsingh's mansion, sending shivers down the spines of the prime minister and his family members. Birshumsher and his brothers were, however, delighted with the news, as this reinforced their belief that the time chosen for his murder was indeed opportune.

On 22 November, during daytime, Birshumsher visited the residence of the prime minister for a farewell call, wherein he was offered the auspicious tika and garland. But taking leave of Runodeepsingh, Birshumsher did not depart for Delhi, but rested under the pavilion set up at his house.

Earlier, Birshumsher and his brothers had asked for some ammunition to take to Delhi where they were expected to join in the fireworks' display. And as Runodeepsingh—the simple-minded man that he was—had not imagined that a fatal conspiracy was being mounted against him by the sons of his own brother, he had sent out a *sannaud* (directive) to the ammunition depot to make available those arms and ammunition. When Birshumsher and his brothers went over to collect the goods, the depot chief, Gen. Ranabirjung Rana, who was a cautious person, said, 'The ammunition cannot be given here, but will be sent after the contingent has passed the Chisapani Gadhi.' This response greatly disappointed Birshumsher and his brothers, as without the weapons and the ammunition their plan would surely have to be aborted. Moreover, as Birshumsher had already bid farewell to the prime minister, he considered it inappropriate to go and meet him again. So from the army headquarters, he fired off a letter to Runodeepsingh, saying, 'What mistrust and injustice on us, the children.' The Shumsher brothers had already won over to their side Runodeepsingh's adviser, Laxmibhakta Poudel. So, as advised by Laxmibhata, Runodeepsingh promptly dispatched another sannaud, asking for the requested goods to be delivered right away. As nobody dared to disobey Runodeepsingh, Padmajung Rana, who happened to be manning the depot at the time, possibly because of Gen. Ranabirjung's absence, duly followed the instructions and delivered the weapons and ammunition. But after giving them away, Padmajung remained uneasy with himself all day. That evening, he visited Ranabirjung Rana's residence to convey all that had happened during the day. Alarmed by the story, Ranabirjung told his brother: 'If one of us doesn't go to stay at Narayanhity tonight, most likely the old man [Runodeepsingh] will be killed.' Here, while the prediction of disaster might have been true, the fact was that, unfortunately, neither of the brothers spent the night at Runodeepsingh's place, nor was any security arrangement bolstered there.

As for Birshumsher and his brothers, as soon as they got hold of the weapons, they promptly distributed them to the soldiers of the contingent assembled at Tundikhel en route to Delhi. While distributing the weapons, the officers instructed the soldiers: 'Nobody gets out of his tent; all are departing early at night; there will be no bugle sounded; only the sound of pipes will be heard; as soon as that sound is heard, just march on to depart, without any delay.' The reason behind not sounding the bugle was that the Shumsher brothers thought it might produce unexpected noise that might be heard by other soldiers, leading to an obstruction in the execution of their plan. After giving out the instructions, Birshumsher and his five brothers returned to the shelter of tents at the former's mansion, leaving Col. Fatteshumsher Rana at the parade ground.

In the Nepalese month of Kartik (October–November), Runodeepsingh usually spent his evenings inscribing 'Ramnam' (a word of prayer dedicated to the Hindu god Ram) on the leaves of tulsi until nine. The Shumsher brothers were well aware of this and planned to enter his mansion before nine in their bid to end his life. To assist them in the task, they had called their maternal uncle Kesharsingh Thapa to their residence, asking him to arrive there at 8 p.m. For a while, the Shumsher brothers waited for him, then they received a message saying that he had fallen off the stairs, and so would not be able to come. 'What do we do now; has our maternal uncle betrayed us?' Birshumsher asked of his brothers. 'If this night is wasted without us doing anything, tomorrow we will all be hung on the trees,' said Gen. Khadgashumsher spiritedly. At this, Chandrashumsher rose to his feet and remarked: 'Either you rule over Hastinapur or dwell under the turf.' All the brothers felt encouraged by this dictum and, reaffirming their resolve, went out of the tent.

Gen. Dhojnarsingh Rana, Runodeepsingh's principal aide, used to come to sleep at Narayanhity at some point between nine and ten. The Shumsher brothers feared that if he arrived early, there was a fairly good chance that their plan would be scuttled. So, one of the brothers, Ranashumsher Rana, was deputed to hold Dhojnarsingh back at his residence, and if possible, get him drunk. From Birshumsher's mansion to Runodeepsingh's, it was about five minutes' distance on foot. In no time, Birshumsher and his four brothers arrived at the gate of the prime minister's residence.

They gained entry under the pretext that an important letter from the British had to be immediately submitted to the prime minister. Once inside, Birshumsher headed to the chamber of

King Prithvibirbikram Shah to hold him there. En route, Col. Chandrashumsher withdrew from the mission, saying, 'My wife is pregnant, so I don't want to kill the old man' (there existed a superstitious belief that one shouldn't kill when one had a baby coming); he, however, stated that if Dhoj were to arrive, he would 'take care of him'. The other brothers now arrived at the section of the servant guards where they encountered Gambhir Katuwal, who was all alone. Gambhir, of course, had already been won over to the side of the Shumsher brothers. As expected, the section had been cleared of the guards—some of them sent out to have their evening meal, while others had been dispatched to perform avoidable responsibilities, and all of them had earlier deposited their weapons in a closed room. Thus, the three Shumsher brothers made it to the first floor of the mansion without much difficulty.

Now Dambershumsher, Khadgashumsher and Bhimshumsher climbed the stairs towards the rooms. Runodeepsingh's room was closed. On knocking, the door opened; the philosopher prime minister was as usual scribbling the sacred letter, bending over the basil leaves. He saw his three nephews enter his room, carrying rifles. It was about 9 p.m. Sitting erect, he asked in fear: 'Why are you here at night, all of a sudden?' The Shumsher brothers chose not to respond verbally. All three opened fire at Runodeepsingh, one shot each—as if that was the real reply to his question. The second shot fired by Khadgashumsher proved to be decisive, taking Runodeepsingh's life.

It is said that, later, Khadgashumsher would often say: 'I conquered Nepal in an hour by firing one bullet.' He could not have been truer. Within an hour of the assassination of the prime minister, the 2000 soldiers assembled at Tundikhel were instructed to raise the slogan of 'Long Live Maharaja Birshumsher', in order to establish him as the all-powerful autocrat of Nepal.

(2)

Accomplishing their mission, Dambershumsher, Khadgashumsher and Bhimshumsher came downstairs, briefly halting at the main gate. Some twenty of Runodeepsingh's armed bodyguards arrived there to join them. Chandrashumsher left almost immediately for Tundikhel in order to command the soldiers assembled there. Birshumsher was at the place of the second queen mother, King Prithvibirbikram Shah's mother. Dambershumsher and Bhimshumsher now arrived at the entrance of her chambers and waited for Birshumsher to come out. The youngest queen mother, the second queen mother's sister, had been party to the conspiracy. So she too was visiting the second queen mother, along with Upendrabikram Shah. The chambers of King Prithvibirbikram and his mother ran along the same corridor that housed the chamber of Runodeepsingh at the Narayanhity mansion. So the news of the prime minister having been shot dead reached there in no time. Issuing orders to set the Saalebom Carriage ready for the king's departure, all three Shumshers came down to the courtyard along with the infant king.

Usually, whenever the king or the prime minister left or returned to the mansion, there would be around one hundred rifle-bearing soldiers, stationed at the courtyard round the clock, ready to salute them. This time, Lt Narbirsingh Basnet was the officer in charge of these soldiers. He was in a kind of fix, having suddenly heard about the prime minister being murdered and now seeing King Prithvibirbikram Shah, accompanied by the queen mother, getting ready to leave their mansion at night, along with Birshumsher. Upon seeing the king, a royal salute was offered by the soldiers. Then all four—the queen mother, Birshumsher, Dambershumsher and Bhimshumsher—took their seats in the carriage beside the monarch. Once inside the carriage, the queen mother turned to Narbirsingh and asked him to come along too. About a year ago, Narbirsingh had served as Dhirshumsher's bodyguard. So he was kind of attached to Dhirshumsher's sons; and now, here was the queen mother commanding him, which he obviously could not afford to disobey. So, along with the soldiers under his command, he marched on, ahead of the carriage.

The main entrance to Runodeepsingh's mansion stood exactly where the old gate is today on the southern side of the Narayanhity Royal Palace. Here at the entrance, Khadgashumsher and his other brothers waited for Birshumsher, and on arrival of the king's carriage, they too mounted it. The carriage now turned westward. Arriving at the turn of the present-day Kesharmahal, there was some commotion. Yet the carriage smoothly rolled on to finally halt under the *khariko bote*, a huge tree standing as the city's landmark at the centre of the Tundikhel parade ground. As per instructions given earlier, pipes were now played at the tents which housed the soldiers bound for Delhi, and all marched out in a file towards the tree. The queen mother now addressed the assembly of soldiers:

> Brothers,
>
> Just tonight, Gore (Gen. Ranabirjung Rana) came over and killed his uncle Runodeepsingh. He is trying to take over the rule by deposing my infant son, King Prithvibirbikram Shah, and replacing him on the throne by the princess, the daughter of the senior queen mother, without the slightest regard to my honour. Because Birshumsher defended the person and the throne of the infant king, besides protecting my honour and dignity, I have bestowed on him the title of Maharaja as well as the entire authority of the office of the prime minister, as was acquired by my father; you all should obey his instructions, which will be in the interest and welfare of all of us.

The queen mother's brief address over, Khadgashumsher shouted out the order of 'salute' to the soldiers, so as to honour Birshumsher, the new Maharaja. However, the soldiers did not respond. Birshumsher and his accomplices were shocked. At this, the queen mother, first raising the pitch of her voice but later moaning with tearful eyes, went on to express her complaints against Ranabirjung Rana. The soldiers were clearly in a state of confusion; yet, complying with the wishes of the queen mother, they finally did honour Birshumsher by offering him a salute. And when an excited Khadgashumsher exhorted loudly, 'Maharaja Birshumsher', the soldiers responded with 'May he live long'. Obviously, now the joy of Birshumsher and his cronies knew no bounds.

However, even though Birshumsher Rana now had on his side the king, the other members of the royal family and over 2000 soldiers, he still had some problems to surmount. There still existed the risk of the arsenal and ammunition falling into the hands of his adversaries, who could then control the majority of the country's troops. Birshumsher's immediate attention was on the artillery section situated near Tundikhel, where Capt. Dhokal Thapa was in charge. Around midnight, Dhokal was summoned, and he presented himself before Birshumsher literally trembling with fear. However, Birshumsher told him, 'You have now become a colonel.' An overjoyed Dhokal bowed in acknowledgement and respect; later, he opened the gates of his office to Birshumsher. Now Birshumsher was without worries; it was after this assumption of control over the arsenal that Birshumsher truly felt that he had become the most powerful man in the country.

Now, under the protection of the more than 2000 soldiers assembled at Tundikhel, and along with the king and the queen mothers, Birshumsher arrived at Upendrabikram Shah's Baag mansion at night. The contingent was also carrying some cannons along. It was well-nigh impossible for Upendrabikram to put up even the slightest hint of opposition. Thereafter, work began on assignments and deputations aimed at exterminating the different groups of Birshumsher's adversaries. Meanwhile, before midnight, a nineteen-gun salute was fired at Tundikhel announcing the arrival of the new Maharaja; thus, the inhabitants of the valley had now no difficulty whatsoever in knowing that significant political changes had occurred in the country.

Meanwhile, Col. Devibahadur Sijapati, who had been held under military detention by Runodeepsingh for some offence, was released and entrusted with the responsibility of taking the lifeless body of the former prime minister to Aryaghat for the cremation rites. Then, Chandrashumsher was deputed to call on the royal preceptor Lokraj Pande, in order to establish control at the army headquarters.

Where the Kesharmahal stands today, there stood the mansions of Gen. Kedarnarsingh and Dhojnarsingh. Dhojnarsingh, Runodeepsingh's adopted son, used to come every night between nine and ten, to sleep at his godfather's residence. So, Ranashumsher was sent to hold Dhojnarsingh back at his mansion for some time. The orders were that, should Dhojnarsingh dare to venture out of his mansion, he was to be shot; it was Capt. Faudsingh Khatri who was given the charge of shooting. But as there was some kind of an uproar at Dhojnarsingh's residence following the assassination of Runodeepsingh, it was presumed that he too had been taken care of. So both Faudsingh and Ranashumsher returned to Tundikhel.

In fact that evening, Dhojnarsingh was inebriated. Yet, the commotion outside drew his attention, and he watched out of the window; the sky was brightly lit by the moon and he could see clearly all around. The sight of the king's Saalebom Carriage bearing the sun-and-moon national flag as well as the emblem of the Maharaja indeed startled him. From his window, he recognized clearly that the queen mothers and the Birshumsher brothers were inside the carriage. And as there was no trace of Runodeepsingh, Dhojnarsingh was in no doubt that his godfather had been assassinated. Since Birshumsher and his brothers were not alone but accompanied by the king and other members of the royal family, he thought that opening fire would not be the right thing to do. But he still wanted to stir up some trouble and so fired from his pistol at the horses. He was off the mark, but it did trigger firing from the royal carriage in reply. The bullet fired from the carriage brushed the sleeve of Dhojnarsingh's shirt and hit the wall behind. Now the only choice Dhojnarsingh had was to flee, which he did, and arriving at the place of his brother, Gen. Kedarnarsingh, he recounted all that he had seen.

At the time when Gen. Birshumsher was receiving the guard of honour of the Maharaja at Tundikhel, Kedarnarsingh and Dhojnarsingh were deliberating upon their future. They decided that the wisest course would be to seek refuge at the British residency, carrying with them all their jewellery. Thus, they entered the residency the same night. Since envoy Col. Berkley was in India on a vacation, the civil surgeon Dr Gimlette was in charge. From Kedarnarsingh and Dhojnarsingh, the acting envoy got a detailed account of the bloody coup. Thereafter, the gates of the residency were left open for more refugees.

When Dhojnarsingh had arrived at Kedarnarsingh's residence, he had found Siddhibir Mathema chatting with his brother, having arrived there earlier. Dhojnarsingh had then asked Siddhibir—who was the son of Capt. Bishnubir, a trusted civil servant of Runodeepsingh's—to also take refuge at the residency as soon as possible, bringing along with him Haripriya, Runodeepsingh's widow. But when Siddhibir went over to Bombay Chowk to fetch Haripriya, he found her giving out orders, herself sporting the three-moon headband of the Maharaja and the prime minister. He saw her calling Col. Gambhir Katuwal to her side, instructing him to ensure that all the attendants 'stayed together in a position of strength'. Long ago, Jungbahadur Rana had pulled out a red-sealed edict of the king, which said that 'in case of the assassination of the Maharaja, his wife should rule, wearing the three-moon headband'. Based on this edict, the senior queen mother had prompted Haripriya to wear the Maharaja's headdress. The two of them believed that at the break of dawn, they would be able to solicit help from Jungbahadur's sons in making an attempt at crushing the conspiracy of the Shumsher brothers. However, they were stunned on hearing from Siddhibir that both Dhojnarsingh and Kedarnarsingh had already sought refuge at the residency. Adding to their disappointment were the reports that their security guards had left their positions. Now they had no alternative but to enter the residency themselves, which they both did, with help from Gambhir Katuwal and Siddhibir Mathema.

The evening after handing over the ammunition to the soldiers bound for Delhi, Padmajung Rana and Ranabirjung Rana had rightly predicted that if one of them didn't stay at the prime minister's place that night he would most likely be killed. However, it was their inability to be there at the prime minister's place that paved the way for the upheaval which took place in Nepal's political landscape.

Col. Harkajung Rana was one of the officers bound for Delhi. He was at Tundikhel when he heard the news of the assassination of Runodeepsingh. On horseback, he rushed to Thapathali where he conveyed the details of what he had heard to the brothers Padmajung Rana and Ranabirjung Rana. Thereafter, in order to report to his eldest brother Jagatjung about the incident, he had galloped towards the Manohara Palace, about two miles away. Meanwhile, Ranabirjung had made a dash towards the ammunition depot with a view to gaining control over it; however, to his utter dismay, he had found that he was too late—Birshumsher had already got the depot under his control.

While returning, Ranabirjung had called on his nephew Yuddhapratapjung in order to ask the latter to go over to Padmajung's place for urgent consultations. During the discussion, Ranabirjung had stated: 'The three of us have about three hundred rifles, and ammunition that will last the whole night. In the event of an attack by the enemies, we can fight all night. After daybreak however, we will let the people decide.' However, since Gen. Padmajung Rana was extremely well off financially, he was of the opinion that it would be imprudent to follow the path of clash and conflict—he wanted his riches to be preserved. So Padmajung counselled his elder brother Ranabirjung and nephew Yuddhapratapjung that a timely escape would serve everyone's interests. In the end, the three resolved to enter the British residency.

However, they didn't have much time to make their escape. Both Ranabirjung and Yuddhapratapjung rushed to their mansions in order to collect the possessions that they wanted to carry with them. With two boxes stacked with jewellery, other ornaments, and Indian currency then worth ten million rupees, Padmajung Rana came down to the garden of his mansion carrying a loaded pistol, surrounded by four armed guards, with his belongings being carried by two attendants. Ranabirjung and Yuddhapratapjung joined him in the garden. Ranabirjung had hurried down carrying a garland of sapphire and other jewellery worth around Rs 20,000; he was also carrying a pistol. In the excitement, Yuddhapratapjung had returned only with a pistol, having forgotten to pick up other personal belongings. Exiting from their garden compound through its sewage conduit that joined a brook outside, all three descended on the rice fields of Kuriagaun village.

At Kuriagaun, Yuddhapratapjung suddenly realized that he was empty-handed. 'I forgot to bring the jewellery and cash. I will go back to bring them,' he said. But Ranabirjung and Padmajung did not want any further delay. Both felt that they were being shadowed by a black ghost in the form of Birshumsher. So Padmajung told his nephew: 'Don't go, it's dangerous; you will not be able to return; we will share whatever we have.' Unconvinced by the assurances of his uncle, the twenty-year-old Yuddhapratapjung retraced his steps towards his mansion. As for Padmajung and Ranabirjung, passing through the countryside, past the temple of Tundaldevi, they arrived at the British residency, heaving a sigh of relief. At daybreak, Narendrabikram Shah also entered the embassy compound, in a landau.

Meanwhile, three battalions, each of fifty armed soldiers and led by an officer, had been sent to kill the three generals who had reportedly gathered at the Thapathali palace. The news was that two of these generals had already fled, while the third one was heading out from Padmajung's garden. Thus, Col. Lalitmansingh Basnet, whose brief was to handle Yuddhapratapjung, waylaid him at Kuriagaun itself. Realizing that there was no way he could escape from the situation, Yuddhapratapjung threw himself at the feet of Lalitmansingh, pleading to him to save his life: 'I have done no harm, don't kill me. Take me to Birshumsher, my uncle.' However, Lalitmansingh ignored the plea and went on to brutally behead Yuddhapratapjung. Also put to death were his load carriers. With Yuddhapratapjung's head as well as the box of his jewellery, Lalitmansingh presented himself before Birshumsher the same night. A delighted Birshumsher returned part of the jewellery as baksheesh to his maternal uncle. Then, Yuddhapratap's decapitated head was sent to Thapathali to be cremated with fanfare.

That night, Gen. Amarjung Rana was staying at Sankhamool where the next day he was to dedicate to the public the newly built pilgrim's home. Soldiers were sent to put him to death; they arrived at Sankhamool that night itself. However, the general was the first one to fire, inflicting injuries on two soldiers and sending the others scurrying around. Amarjung's familiarity with the lanes of Lalitpur now came in handy. Running through those lanes, he headed towards the south, finally arriving at Maakalkhucha to heave a sigh of relief. Amarjung then planned to escape to India, along with Shyamdutta Pandit; but the next day itself he was captured at Thegan, put in chains, and imprisoned in the forest of Nagarjun outside Kathmandu.

Meanwhile, as soon as Birshumsher entered the Baag mansion, he sent for his preceptor Lokraj Pande. So far, he had not given any thought to getting rid of Jagatjung, who was being held under house arrest. But now, Lokraj advised him: 'No, we can't keep him alive, that will be dangerous.' Thus, early the next morning a troop of a hundred soldiers under the command of Col. Uttardhoj Adhikari and Col. Faudsingh Khatri was sent to Manohara Palace to finish off Jagatjung. Jagatjung had found out about Runodeepsingh's death through Harkajung Rana who had rushed to Manohara before midnight. Jagatjung had also heard the sound of the nineteen-gun salute fired in honour of the new Maharaja. However, he did not expect any harm to come to himself: 'Nothing untoward may happen to someone like me who is resigned to a quiet life. What harm have I done?' When the troop led by Col. Uttardhoj Adhikari and Col. Faudsingh Khatri arrived at Jagatjung's place in the morning, they asked him to come down to the courtyard. But while he was climbing down the stairs, a soldier, Kabiraj Thapa, shot him from below. Tottering, Jagatjung fell on the floor, and while his blood-soaked body trembled with pain, another soldier was asked to cut the head of the half-dead body.

Philosophically speaking, fate indeed takes strange twists and turns. The Ranas had succeeded in taking control over the powers and authority of the kingdom, thanks to the political acumen, sagacity and skills of Jungbahadur. But now, the loyal soldiers of the same Ranas were merrily returning to Kathmandu, carrying the blood-soaked head of Jungbahadur's eldest son; he had been done to death as if to reward his innocence. Birshumsher was gleeful when he saw the lifeless head of Jagatjung. Then, Jagatjung's mortal remains were burned after 4 p.m. that day after some delay in taking his decapitated head to Manohara.

Meanwhile, Gen. Lalitjung, Jungbahadur's son from his mistress, and a few other courtiers, had hid themselves inside toilets. But at daybreak, they were arrested and imprisoned. That morning, Birshumsher called to his palace all those officers who had pledged their loyalty to him by placing coins at his feet. He also took the salute accorded to the Maharaja from the soldiers assembled in Kathmandu for the morning parade. He was now clearly the undisputed ruler of the country.

The same morning, Padmajung Rana sent his brother Gen. Jitjung in Calcutta a telegram giving the details of the killings in Kathmandu. As for the British residency, the previous night the acting Resident had reported the happenings to the secretary of the governor general. Then, Birshumsher, in his capacity as the prime minister, wrote a letter to the British residency asking that Ranabirjung and others be handed over to the Nepalese kingdom. 'They are all culprits,' he stated in the letter. However, Gimlette chose not to reply to the letter as there was no intention to hand over the refugees. Yet, in order to be informed about all that had happened, he went over to the Baag mansion in the evening. And as Gimlette was telling Birshumsher and his brothers that Padmajung Rana and others had sought refuge at the residency and that Haripriya, Runodeepsingh's widow, too, was one of the refugees, suddenly and unexpectedly Gambhir Katuwal showed up in the room. An astonished Gimlette turned to Gambhir and asked in Hindi, 'What, Katuwal! You were also there, weren't you? Why have you returned?' Birshumsher was utterly dismayed at this turn of events.

Meanwhile, at Runodeepsingh's mansion, the three-moon headband of the Maharaja had gone missing—it was being searched for, but had not been found yet. The general assumption was that Haripriya had taken it away with her. This assumption now turned out to be correct. Birshumsher came to know that Gambhir Katuwal had taken Haripriya, with the three-moon headband in tow, to the residency. He was enraged but could not express his anger in the presence of the envoy. Once the envoy left, Birshumsher looked for excuses to punish the colonel who had greatly contributed to the successful execution of the intrigue of the Shumsher brothers. So on that same day, Gambhir was forced out of the valley, after being accused of being 'an ungrateful person' who could not be forgiven for his complicity in the murder of Runodeepsingh, especially because he was his bodyguard. He was also denied the promised baksheesh of Rs 50,000. But Laxmibhakta Poudel got his baksheesh as promised; he also retained his job for nearly three years.

That day, Birshumsher sent out a sannaud to the heads of all districts and passes in the kingdom. And now since it was clear as day that Gen. Ranabirjung had not been involved in the conspiracy, Birshumsher thought it improper to apportion any blame on him. Briefly, the message read:

> . . . Salute to all. Maharaja Runodeepsingh Rana has left us for the heavenly abode. To free the culprit Jagatjung from house arrest, his brothers as well as Kedarnarsingh, Amarjung and Dhojnarsingh made an attempt on the life of the King, while also assailing the dignity, honour and the person of the second Queen Mother. As we successfully protected the person,

the throne and the honour, we have received from the King through the red seal the powers and authority bestowed on Jungbahadur, along with the title of Maharaja. Henceforth, should you obey the laws and perform as directed by us in this sannaud, your works will be reported to the administration accordingly. But if we find that our orders are disobeyed, we will act as per our decision. So act dutifully. If any one of the culprits like Gen. Padmajung, Gen. Ranabirjung, Gen. Kedarnarsingh, Amarjung and Dhojnarsingh—they were all trying to help Jagatjung—pass through your way, arrest him, and putting him in chains, send him to us here. Keep all your soldiers alert and vigilant.

Dated: 23 November 1885

Part 1 was published in the monthly magazine *Sharada* (Issue II) under the title 'He who has the word has the Palace', in 1957

Part 2, unpublished, was written possibly in 1958 under the title 'Conspiracy of the Year AD 1885 and the Murder of Runodeepsingh Rana'

Eleven

Maharaja Devshumsher Is Deposed and Banished

Following the brutal murder of Runodeepsingh, General Birshumsher Kunwar Rana became the prime minister of Nepal, also assuming the title of Shree Teen Maharaja as the King of Kaski and Lamjung provinces. Before long, he revised the roll of succession that gave his brothers their turn to succeed him. He also introduced the practice of adding the title of Jung Bahadur to his own and his brothers' surnames as a grateful tribute to the late Jungbahadur Kunwar Rana, who had instituted the Rana's family rule in the kingdom.

In the revised roll based on seniority in age, Birshumsher, thirty-three, was at the top. Following him in order were Lt Gen. Dambershumsher, twenty-six, Gen. Khadgashumsher, twenty-four, Gen. Ranashumsher, twenty-three, Gen. Devshumsher, twenty-three, Gen. Chandrashumsher, twenty-two, and Col. Bhimshumsher, twenty.

Likewise, his other brothers, namely Col. Fatteshumsher, twenty, Gen. Lalitshumsher, seventeen, Gen. Jitshumsher, seventeen, Col. Purnashumsher, fourteen, Col. Yadushumsher, thirteen, Col. Durgashumsher, eleven, Col. Shershumsher, ten, Col. Juddhashumsher, ten, Col. Khambashumsher, ten, and Col. Harshashumsher, ten, figured in the roll. Denied the turn to succeed him and therefore a place in the roll were his minor brothers who had not come of age. Birshumsher and his sixteen brothers were famously called the Seventeen-Brothers Ranajee.

Birshumsher also appointed Damber as his principal aide, Khadga as the commander-in-chief of the army, Ranashumsher as commander-general of the west, Devshumsher as commander-general of the south, Chandra as commander-general of the east, and Bhim as commander-general of the north.

For almost a year, the roll of succession was upheld and heeded. Birshumsher was generally grateful to his brothers, particularly to Khadga, for the parts they played in his rise to the high pedestal of state power. On his part, Khadga had entertained the hope that Birshumsher, apart from being delighted with the premiership as well as the title of royalty, would also recognize his younger brother's contribution, and oblige by vesting him with some executive powers. But Birshumsher was reluctant to hand over the authority the brother expected and only gave him the charge of some civil works. Naturally, Khadga remained dissatisfied and disgruntled with his brother.

Initially, Khadga discharged his petty responsibilities honestly, but in due course he grew arrogant and ambitious. He began to ignore the prime minister, never taking him into confidence—not even bothering to apprise him of major developments occurring in his domain.

Khadga took pride in his role in his family's usurpation of state authority. He had fired the first fatal bullet at his uncle and then prime minister Runodeepsingh Kunwar Rana, clearing the deck for Birshumsher to succeed him. He often bragged about it, saying, 'I got it [state power] for him by firing a single bullet, and in an hour.' So he was disinclined to wait his turn that would come only after the death of his elder brother—a considerably long time away. Driven by an irresistible desire to become Nepal's prime minister himself, Khadga began internal manoeuvrings to remove his brother Bir.

Khadga told his other brothers how Birshumsher had been ungrateful by disregarding his role and contribution. Word spread about Khadga being disillusioned with his elder brother, which led to Birshumsher also starting to harbour doubts and suspicion about what the army commander-in-chief was up to. One day, all of a sudden, Bir fired all the civil servants belonging to Khadga's camp, replacing them with people he trusted.

Two women, Kanchi Maiya and her sister Chirbire Maiya (daughters of ex-prime minister Jungbahadur Rana), had also played a crucial role in the murder of Runodeepsingh. Both had been sufficiently rewarded for their contribution, yet both were far from being happy and satisfied. All along, they had wanted to have some say in running the day-to-day administration of the country. On his part, however, Bir warned them against any attempt at interfering in state affairs. Also joining the disgruntled women's group was Kahili Maiya, one of Khadga's sisters. Now all three began to meet Khadga more frequently, and one evening they resolved to depose Bir at all costs.

Bir had successfully built a strong and powerful spy organization. He had moles at the residences of each of his brothers. One day his spies told him that some high state officials had begun gathering at Khadga's residence, and in the process had even missed functions where their presence was mandatory, such as the one that accorded daily salute to the prime minister. A furious Bir began investigating, and found out that Sirdar Haribhakta and Sirdar Bhaktabahadur, senior civil servants said to be close to Khadga, were the offenders. The duo was fired, and it became obvious that it wouldn't be long before Khadga too lost his job.

Bir's move further annoyed the commander-in-chief, and his disillusionment snowballed. He began working overtime to remove his brother and even created a clandestine organization of his own towards this end. It is said that his younger brother Chandrashumsher, the commander-general of the east, and the younger queen mother Bishnudibyeswori were brought in as members of the secret clique.

Khadga had fixed the date for solemnizing his stepbrother Col. Shershumsher's bratabandha in the third week of February 1888. This was after Prime Minister Birshumsher returned from Calcutta, where he had paid a visit at the invitation of the British government of India. A plot was hatched to invite Birshumsher to Khadga's Thapathali Palace, seize him forcibly and depose him right there. Accordingly, an invitation to Bir was duly extended.

Before he left for the Thapathali Palace, Bir's principal aide and bodyguard, Faudsingh Khatri, alerted him about Khadga's dubious activities.

'Some untoward accident may occur, so it is better if Your Highness doesn't go there,' he said. However, a confident Bir, who knew quite well that his men were deployed at the palace in great numbers, chose to attend the function; he wouldn't be disappointing his brother by turning down the invitation. Yet, he would visit the place after making adequate preparation.

Security was beefed up at the Thapathali Palace before Bir's arrival, but this raised doubts in Khadga's mind that his brother no longer trusted him. Khadga also felt he was being insulted. Yet, at the palace, a red carpet was rolled out for Bir as he was taken to the drawing room where other invitees had already gathered. All the invitees now sat down for the feast. At this, an intelligence officer in plain clothes sauntered up to whisper something in the ear of the prime minister. Immediately thereafter, another officer submitted to Bir that the main gates of the palace had been closed all of a sudden.

A time-honoured tradition had it that the main gates of the palace should always remain open when a visitor, particularly the prime minister, was in and around. But for some unknown reason, the main gates of the Thapathali Palace were closed soon after the religious function was over, though Birshumsher was still inside. The prime minister smelt a rat. Meanwhile, a third spy came around to announce that host Khadgashumsher had disappeared, and was nowhere to be seen. At this Bir left his food and, washing his hands and mouth swiftly, tried to make his way out of the palace. To his dismay, however, he found the main entrance of the palace closed. An enraged prime minister had to shout at the top of his voice and scold the guards manning the palace gates to finally throw them open. Following the incident, Bir was further incensed with his brother Khadga.

On this side, upon knowing that the prime minister had left his meal midway to leave the palace, Khadgashumsher knew that his brother's suspicions had been aroused. In turn, Khadga also became more suspicious of his brother. It didn't take long for him to realize that his days in the capital, Kathmandu, were numbered.

Before long, the Samyak Pooja, a twelve-yearly religious function of the followers of Buddhism, was organized at the Swayambhu Monastery in the north-west of the capital. Minor king Prithvibirbikram Shah and Prime Minister Birshumsher were scheduled to attend the sacred ceremony. But a plan was afoot to 'forcibly arrest Birshumsher, depose him and send him to exile'. Bir, who got wind of the conspiracy against him from his spies, stayed away.

Khadga's brother Chandrashumsher, commander-general of the east, was an accomplice to this secret plan. After Bir didn't show up at the function, an exasperated Khadga assigned Chandra to go to the Hiti Palace to fetch the prime minister. Chandra went but was held up at the palace and didn't return. While Khadga's conspiracy was aborted, Bir saved himself from a disaster.

That same evening, Prime Minister Bir summoned brother Khadga to Hiti Palace. The commander-in-chief couldn't dare ignore the call from his brother, so riding a horse he swiftly presented himself at the palace. No sooner had he dismounted than Bir's security personnel ringed him. Khadga's bodyguards were disarmed, and it didn't take him long to see why his brother had called him.

Now Prime Minister Bir himself arrived on the scene and told Khadga directly: 'Brother, you have become extremely arrogant and ambitious. You didn't show the patience required to wait for your turn as listed in the order roll, so you are disqualified from the roll. We can't keep you here. Now you should go over to Palpa.' With these words, Khadga was dismissed from the position of commander-in-chief, while also losing his turn to become prime minister.

On hearing about Khadga's arrest, the younger queen mother Bishnudibyeswori had rushed to Bir's palace in an apparent bid to save him. But as soon as she arrived at the venue, a pistol dropped from her waistband on to the ground. Bir had long been looking for a pretext to get rid of her, and now here it was. Carrying a pistol amounted to committing a crime, and she was suspected of being an accomplice in the anti-Bir plot. Disregarding the help she had once rendered to the Bir brothers when they had entered the royal palace to murder Runodeepsingh, and suspecting that her stay in Nepal would create more troubles for them in the future, the queen mother was sent out to exile in Kashi, India. Also convicted of the crime was their maternal uncle Col. Kesharsingh Thapa. He was deported to Salyan district.

Chandrashumsher, commander-general of the east, was also suspected of being involved in the plot at this time. Covert preparations were made to banish him from the capital.

But Devshumsher, commander-general of the south, came around to plead on Chandra's behalf. Bir's second wife, Queen Toyakumari, too, reportedly confronted her husband saying, 'Isn't it enough that the actual culprit is punished? Why become more unpopular by deporting other brothers?' Chandra was lucky to be absolved of the crime.

That same day, following Khadga's deportation, Ranashumsher replaced him as the commander-in-chief, while Devshumsher was appointed as the commander-general of the west.

Barely two months had passed after he became the commander-in-chief when Ranashumsher died unexpectedly at the young age of twenty-five. Devshumsher stepped in as the new commander-in-chief, while Chandrashumsher became the commander-general of the west.

Khadga, deported to Palpa district, was later given the charge of the municipality and appointed the district's governor. Living in the district for a long period of time, he later fled to Sagar town of Madhya Pradesh in India, spending the rest of his life there.

The Ranas were now split into two groups—the Shumsher family and the Jung family—that had an embittered relationship. About a year after Khadga's deportation, the exiled sons of the late Jungbahadur Rana mounted a revolt against Birshumsher. Led by ex-general Ranabirjung and assisted even by some Indian kings, the rebel forces successfully took control over some territories of the Terai region bordering India, while committing acts of looting and arson in Ilam and Dhankuta districts in the east of the country.

In the west of the kingdom, Ranabir himself was active. He planned to take control over Syuraj and Butwal districts, as also to win the Nepalese soldiers there over to his side. But the Nepalese troops that had moved from Kathmandu brutally crushed the rebellion.

Ranabirjung had not lost heart, however. He hatched a plan to deal with Birshumsher when the latter paid a visit to Calcutta at the invitation of the British government. While returning from India, Bir was scheduled to pass by the famous Hindu pilgrimage centre of Kashi. The plan of Ranbirjung and his associates was to attack Bir when he took a holy dip in the sacred Ganges River. Experienced swimmers were commissioned towards this end. But the plot was unearthed in time and Bir saved himself from being drowned.

Prime Minister Birshumsher wanted to marry off his two daughters from his younger wife Topkumari to minor king Prithvibirbikram Shah. He cherished the hope that the offspring from one of his daughters would be the future King of Nepal. But the king's mother, Queen Mother Tarakumari, was opposed to the idea. She herself may have been a daughter of the late Jungbahadur Rana, but as some of her brothers had been murdered, and others subjected to injustice at the hands of the Shumsher Ranas, she had disdain for the Ranas of the Shumsher family and was dead against the proposition of her son marrying into the family. So when Birshumsher left for his visit to Calcutta, the queen mother quietly called two ten-year-old Rajput girls, namely Rebatiraman Rajyalaxmi and Laxmidibyeswori Rajyalaxmi, from the Punjab province of India, solemnizing their marriage with the twelve-year-old

King Prithvibirbikram. Bir found out about the wedding on his return, and was infuriated.

Not long thereafter, Bir forcibly gave the hands of his two daughters, Kirtidibyeswori and Durgadibyeswori, to Prithvibirbikram. Queen Mother Tara opposed Bir's move, but she couldn't do anything. Instead, she ended up paying a price for getting the Rajput girls for her son. Realizing that she would remain a liability even in the future, she was shunted out to exile.

Birshumsher gave strict orders that the king be banned from meeting his queens from India. Obviously, he wanted the future King of Nepal to be born from one of his two daughters who were now wedded to the king. To this end, he appointed a trusted official, giving him the title of Sirdar, for twenty-four-hour surveillance of the royal palace. Notwithstanding all this, the king's interaction with his Rajput queens couldn't be cut off as the adolescent Prithvibirbikram had found a way out. Reportedly, he won the surveillance official over to his side by gifting him a diamond ring, then valued at about one lakh rupees. Consequently, after the death of Birshumsher, the Rajput queen Laxmidibyeswori gave birth to prince Tribhuvanbirbikram Shah who would go on to become the King of Nepal.

It is not that Nepal didn't see some development- and growth-related activities during Bir's administration. For the first time in the capital city Kathmandu, pipelines of drinking water were laid, which came to be called 'Bir water taps'. Later, arrangements for drinking water were also made in the Bhaktapur city. The Bir Hospital, the Bir Library (present-day national archives), the Clock Tower and the Sanskrit Hostel were all his creations for the capital, Kathmandu. He also commissioned the construction of the ornate building of the Hiti Palace, his personal residence, near the Narayanhity Royal Palace.

Though an autocrat, Jungbahadur Rana had imposed severe restrictions on his brothers stacking the nation's wealth in foreign banks. His successor, the pacifist, religious-minded and childless Runodeepsingh, never ever thought of amassing wealth. But Birshumsher was different: his name goes down in Nepalese history as someone who started the practice of plundering the nation's wealth. During his administration, the practice of misusing state income as personal property was encouraged. Bir and his brothers amassed wealth also by registering the fertile arable land of the Terai in their names as personal property. The riches thus amassed were kept in banks outside Nepal—Bir himself had taken the initiative towards this end. While the king was still young and nobody else was in a position to raise his voice against such excesses, Bir had no qualms about looting the nation.

After being the prime minister and the Shree Teen Maharaja for about fifteen years and eight months, Birshumsher died at age forty-eight, presumably of high blood pressure, on 5 March 1901. When he assumed office, he was followed in the order of succession by his brothers Khadgashumsher, Ranashumsher and Devshumsher. But by this time, Khadga had been sent into exile and Ranashumsher had died. So Devshumsher, the youngest of the three, became the prime minister.

In acquiring the premiership as well as the title of kingship, Devshumsher also followed the practice of forcing the adolescent monarch to affix the imprint of his palm on the inheritance document. Thereafter, Chandrashumsher was promoted to the position of commander-in-chief of the army, and Bhimshumsher as a high-ranking military personnel.

Prime Minister Devshumsher turned out to be a simple-minded and benevolent person. He harboured a progressive outlook aimed at promoting the interests of the country, the crown and the common people. He had seen and been impressed by the industrial growth in England and Japan, and believed that the living standard of the Nepalese people could be raised, just like that of the Japanese people. So soon after he assumed state authority, he began launching programmes designed to introduce reforms. To this end, he appointed his nephew Gehendrashumsher Rana (Bir's eldest son) as his principal adviser.

Devshumsher wanted to give back the kings of the Shah dynasty their legitimate rights. He wanted to exercise premiership under the guidance of the monarch. For the country, he wanted a representative advisory council—in line with what they had in England—to run the affairs of the state. He contemplated acquiring the service of foreign experts for this purpose. Domestically, he installed suggestion boxes to solicit views and opinions in this regard at different places in the Kathmandu valley. Those who were afraid to give out their name for fear of retribution could remain anonymous. On 27 May 1901, a weekly newspaper named *Gorkhapatra* was launched, aimed at informing the people about the important developments in the kingdom as well as outside. He had even sought the suggestions of Jayaprithvibahadur Singh, the King of Bajhang district, in this regard. Dev also emphasized the spread of education in the country, opening more than one hundred Nepali-medium schools across the kingdom, all at once. The very first school for girls in Nepal was opened during his administration.

Cottage industries designed to promote industry and commerce were also initiated, while civil servants got their working hours fixed from 10 a.m. to 5 p.m., and they were also entitled to regular holidays. Furthermore, Devshumsher began efforts towards the eradication of slavery in Nepal.

On 27 May 1901, Devshumsher convened a special meeting of the Courtiers' Council, to which he invited army officers, administrative officials, businessmen and prominent people from various walks of life. The participants discussed a number of issues at the six-hour-long meeting with emphasis on the development of rural industries. However, the meeting, unprecedented in the Rana administration, angered the Ranas who were averse to change.

Dev's successor Chandra felt that the progressive work started by his brother would spread awareness among the general populace, but would backfire on his own interests and those of his brothers'. Assuming that the so-called progress programmes would spell disaster for his brothers and cousins in the future, Chandra began to plot against his brother, forgetting that the same brother had once saved him from being sent into exile. He told his brother Fatteshumsher, who was next in line of succession, that continuing with Dev's liberal policy would mean a reversal of the situation wherein the Nepalese people followed the leadership of the Ranas. Initially, Fatteshumsher disagreed, but eventually he gave in.

On 27 June 1901, Chandra and his brothers resolved to carry out their plan of deposing the prime minister. Under the plan, Devshumsher would be led to the Hiti Palace where he would be arrested forcibly. Astrologers were asked to predict the propitious hour for the task. The prime minister was giving away medals and prizes to outstanding students at a function held at the local Durbar High School. The prize distribution over, Devshumsher was reminded that he was scheduled to pay a visit to the Hiti Palace to help sort out the property dispute of his nephews, Birshumsher's sons. Dev's intervention in the property dispute was a mere pretext designed to drag him to the palace where a plot to arrest him had been hatched. Unable to decline his brothers' request, Devshumsher went over to Hiti. On entering the palace he saw his nephews arguing. But no sooner had he entered the drawing room than Fatteshumsher, Durgashumsher and Gehendrashumsher seized him. Overpowered and tied with the cloth of his waistband, he was shoved to the floor. Dev's bodyguard, Col. Indrabahadur Shahi, trained his gun on the commander-in-chief Chandra, but Bhimshumsher pulled the gun away from behind him at that very moment, rendering the bodyguard helpless. Indrabahadur was arrested immediately, while Devshumsher was forcibly taken as a prisoner.

After realizing that he had fallen into a trap, Devshumsher said, 'Brothers, I am sorry. I didn't know; it was my mistake. Henceforth, I will do as you all want me to do. So forgive me, and let me go free.' But his plea was a cry in the wilderness. Commander-in-Chief Chandra and his cohorts remained unmoved.

The adolescent king Prithvibirbikram Shah was brought to the scene almost immediately. On seeing the plight of Prime Minister Devshumsher, the monarch asked Chandra and his companions: 'What's happening here? Why have you done this?' Chandra replied, saying, 'Devshumsher could not run the administration of the country effectively. Many people have gotten angry with us because of the work he is carrying out. The nation's resources are being spent wantonly. So we have been forced to arrest him.' Chandra then made a strong plea that Dev be deposed as the prime minister and replaced by himself as it was now his turn, according to the roll of succession. Prithvibirbikram, however, turned down the plea.

By this time, a contingent of the Bijuli battalion had been called to offer the honour salute to the new prime minister, and it had already assembled in the courtyard below. Dismayed by the king's refusal to carry out Chandra's plea, Fatteshumsher walked over to the window overlooking the courtyard. Addressing the army contingent below, he said, 'We are deposing Devshumsher; Chandrashumsher has become the prime minister and Maharaja from today. Offer him the salute.' The commanders of the salute contingent, however, refused to take orders from Fatteshumsher. They said they wouldn't accept Chandra as the prime minister until the king himself said so. Bhimshumsher, disheartened by the army's refusal to obey Fatteshumsher's order, could clearly see that Prithvibirbikram was hesitant. He trained his revolver at the king and said, 'Tell the army officers, and fast. Otherwise, we will be forced to shoot you.' Now the king saw that the Ranas of the Shumsher family had encircled him; so, addressing the salute officers said, 'Yes, I have appointed Chandrashumsher as the prime minister and Maharaja.' Thereafter, the army contingent presented a guard of honour to the new prime minister. A twenty-one-gun salute boomed in the air.

Chandrashumsher was still not confident that his move would go unopposed. He brought King Prithvibirbikram to his palace at Thapathali. Here he asked the king to affix the traditional royal handprint on the official document granting him the position of the prime minister. Here, too, the king was reluctant for a while, until Chandra himself, flashing a pistol in his hand, said, 'Your Majesty, please hurry up with it.' Thus ended the 114-day-rule of Devshumsher.

That very day, Devshumsher, mounted on a palanquin, was exiled to the eastern district of Dhankuta via Bhaktapur and Dhulikhel. Living for about two and a half months in the east, he fled to India via Darjeeling, arriving at Jharipani in north India where he spent the rest of his life.

In the year 1904, Prime Minister Chandrashumsher arrived in Delhi at the invitation of the British government. He was scheduled to return via Benaras, home to the traditional Hindu pilgrimage site. It is said that Devshumsher and his supporters had worked out a plan to kill Chandra and thus take revenge for their deportation. The British government, however, got wind of the plot with the result that Devshumsher was put under house arrest during Chandra's visit.

Devshumsher bought a big house in Benaras, aimed at running a school and a hostel for Nepalese students arriving there for higher studies. He also instituted a permanent fund worth about four lakh Indian rupees to support the educational facilities. His plan was not realized, however, as no one came forward to take charge of running the school, thanks largely to the threat doled out by Prime Minister Chandrashumsher. A disappointed Devshumsher later transferred the fund money to an orphanage in England.

Thirteen years into exile, Maharaja Devshumsher died on 20 January 1914 in the Indian town of Jharipani.

Unpublished, written in 1960

Calendar of Events

10 January 1775: King Prithvinarayan Shah dies/Pratapsingh Shah ascends the throne

26 January 1775: Coronation of King Pratapsingh Shah

22 June 1775: King Ranabahadur Shah is born

16 December 1777: King Pratapsingh Shah dies/Ranabahadur Shah ascends the throne

 2 September 1778: Bahadur Shah takes over reins of control/ Queen Rajendralaxmi is interned

20 June 1779: Queen Rajendralaxmi returns to power

 4 February 1782: Victory over Siranchowk

29 October 1782: Victory over Lamjung

27 December 1783: Damodar Pande gets the sack/Kazi Bamsaraj Pande exiled again

 9 March 1785: Bamsaraj Pande returns to Kathmandu

21 April 1785: Bamsaraj Pande is beheaded

 2 July 1786: Bahadur Shah is imprisoned again

14 July 1786: Queen Rajendralaxmi dies

23 July 1786: Bahadur Shah becomes mukhtiyar

 4 August 1786: Kazi Swaroopsingh Karki is beheaded

20 June 1792: Chinese troops cross over Kukurghat

20 August 1792: Chinese troops drown in Betravati River

 6 October 1792: Nepal–China Treaty signed

26 June 1794: Ranabahadur Shah regains control

19 February 1797: Bahadur Shah imprisoned again

24 June 1797: Bahadur Shah is murdered

2 October 1797: Prince Girban is born

19 February 1798: Stone inscription of Trust Document placed at the Pashupati Temple

8 March 1798: King Ranabahadur Shah abdicates/Girban ascends the throne

1 November 1799: Queen Kantabati dies

20 January 1800: King Girban taken to Nuwakot

10 May 1800: Ranabahadur Shah flees from Pulchowk

27 May 1800: Ranabahadur Shah arrives in Kashi

28 September 1801: Kazi Kirtimansingh murdered

18 April 1802: Captain Knox arrives in Kathmandu

27 November 1802: Queen Rajrajeswori arrives in Thankot

17 December 1802: Queen Rajrajeswori re-enters palace

18 July 1803: New Courtiers' Council formed

23 July 1803: Captain Knox leaves Kathmandu

1 March 1804 Ranabahadur Shah returns to Kathmandu

7 March 1804: Ranabahadur Shah re-enters the royal palace

13 March 1804: Kazi Damodar Pande is killed

2 February 1805: Rajrajeswori is interned again

4 March 1805: Shah sons (minors) imprisoned

21 May 1805: Rajrajeswori exiled to Helambu

26 February 1806: Ranabahadur Shah assumes the office of mukhtiyar

26 April 1806: Ranabahadur Shah murdered

26 May 1806: Shah sons beheaded

31 May 1806: Thirteen people beheaded en masse

7 December 1813: Crown Prince Rajendra is born

20 November 1816: King Girban dies

6 December 1816: King Rajendra ascends the throne

26 February 1832: Queen Lalittripurasundari dies

31 October 1835: Bhimsen Thapa appointed commander-in-chief

24 July 1837: Prince Devendra Shah dies/Bhimsen Thapa imprisoned

22 July 1839: Bhimsen Thapa slits his own throat

30 July 1839: Bhimsen Thapa dies

5 October 1839: Crown Prince Surendrabikram Shah is born

21 June 1840: Nepalese Army mutinies

20 August 1841: Bhimsen Thapa (his effigy made of the holy shrub kush) is cremated

6 September 1841: Queen Samrajyalaxmi dies

10 November 1842: Crown Prince Surendrabikram Shah assumes special rights

5 January 1843: King Rajendra empowers his queen

17 April 1843: Mathbarsingh Thapa arrives in Kathmandu

13 July 1843: Thapas cleared of charges in the poison case

18 December 1843: Mathbarsingh appointed commander-in-chief

25 November 1844: The Dhukuwabas incident

17 May 1845: Mathbarsingh Thapa is slain

26 May 1845: Queen Rajyalaxmi assumes power

23 September 1845: Fattejung Shah appointed mukhtiyar

14 September 1846: The Kot Massacre

30 October 1846: Crown Prince Surendrabikram Shah assumes the authority to rule

31 October 1846: The Bhandarkhal Episode

23 November 1846: King Rajendra leaves for pilgrimage

11 May 1847: The royal messengers arrested

12 May 1847: King Rajendra deposed/Surendrabikram Shah ascends the throne

27 July 1847: The attack at Sugauli

20 September 1848: Jungbhadur assumes total control

30 November 1847: Crown Prince Trailokya is born

14 May 1848: Jungbahadur takes the title Rana for surname

 7 August 1856: Jungbahadur becomes the King of Kaski and Lamjung Provinces

26 January 1877: Jungbahadur dies

30 March 1878: Crown Prince Trailokya dies

17 May 1881: King Surendra dies/Prithvibirbikram Shah enthroned

12 July 1881: King Rajendra dies

14 January 1882: Runodeepsingh returns from the Terai

14 October 1884: Commander-in-Chief Dhirshumsher dies

22 November 1885: Runodeepsingh is assassinated

 5 March 1901: Birshumsher dies

27 May 1901: Devshumsher convenes special meeting of the Courtiers' Council

27 June 1901: Chandrashumsher appointed prime minister

20 January 1914: Maharaja Devshumsher dies in India

Index